THE SELF-ESTE

How to Discover and Raise Your Self-Esteem and Confidence, Cultivate Feelings of Self-Worth and Love Yourself

By

Tiffany White

DISCLAIMER

FOREWORD

First, I will like to thank you for taking the first step of trusting me and deciding to purchase/read this life-transforming eBook. Thanks for spending your time and resources on this material.

I can assure you of exact results if you will diligently follow the exact blueprint I lay bare in the information manual you are currently reading. It has transformed lives, and I strongly believe it will equally transform your own life too.

All the information I presented in this Do-It-Yourself piece is easy to digest and practice.

BOOK DESCRIPTION

Healthy self-esteem encourages us to use healthy judgment, and feel confident. It additionally benefits us physically. It keeps us away from heart issues, hypertension and even offers vitality to carry out our everyday responsibilities at home. If we have a poor self-esteem, it is undeniably increasingly hard to be persuaded to roll out any improvements throughout our life. Poor self-esteem is frequently the reason behind why we become languid, gorge, settle on poor choices, become discouraged, and experience difficulties. I believe you can review the things we can do to develop self-esteem as examined in this book.

A decent self-esteem is significant for building and keeping up great wellbeing and remaining positive in this day and age. You can figure out how to improve your self-esteem by rehearsing the guides examined in this book. This takes abilities, which you as of now have inside you, and you can figure out how to utilize these aptitudes emphatically. You can truly profit by these procedures by applying positive intuition into your day-by-day schedule. Self-esteem influences numerous parts of our life. We need healthy self-esteem to be fruitful and to like whom we are. Self-esteem is the establishment of our certainty and the manner in which we see ourselves.

In this book, you'll learn how to discover and raise your self-esteem and confidence, cultivate feelings of self-worth and love yourself in order for you to live a happy life. You'll also explore different suggestions on maintaining self-esteem in a variety of different situations - like dates, job interviews, with a few different ways to begin carrying on with conscious life and more.

TABLE OF CONTENTS

INTRODUCTION

A cheerful life is yours for the taking. Quit being negative and pitiful constantly. Life should be that way. Life should be a great positive thing. We as a whole realize that life is short, so be upbeat and carry on with the belief that you should live. Love yourself as well as other people. Set objectives in each aspect of your life. And after that simply be upbeat. Regardless of what occurs, search for the great and be cheerful. You can have an upbeat life, so take it as of now.

Love yourself and love other individuals more. Try not to harp on terrible past encounters. Consider the majority of the brilliant things about yourself. It might be elusive beneficial things; however, there must be a considerable number of things. Ask some confided-in family or companions, if need be. In any case, don't be so reproachful of yourself. What might you tell your closest companion if they approached you for such a rundown? Presently consider yourself that way and record a rundown. Get out the rundown at whatever point you begin to contemplate yourself and read the rundown so anyone can hear. Watch how you will to begin to have a glad life. Concentrate on other individuals also. Assist them with trip and you won't concentrate on yourself and your very own issues to such an extent. Search for little and huge approaches to be pleasant and help other individuals out as well.

Set a wide range of goals. Set work, family, love life, otherworldly life, recreational, and wellbeing objectives. Make progress toward balance throughout everyday life, but make sure you don't disregard any zone. Set a deadline and don't surrender until you meet your objectives. Try not to be reluctant to flop either, simply attempt once more. You simply find one route not to succeed, that's it in a nutshell. Continue attempting and you will meet your objectives.

Be sure and happy. The main mystery to a cheerful life is being glad and not pitiful. Everything comes down to the psyche. Did you realize that you can pick what you think about? Indeed, you can be glad, yet it is all up to you. Try not to let outside conditions decide your satisfaction. Life isn't reasonable and terrible things happen constantly. In any case, you can't give those things a chance to remove your bliss. Be glad paying little respect to the conditions. Realize that a light lies ahead and be cheerful about that. Think positive contemplations consistently.

It's my aim to have each book I compose finish up with some move you can make today to put the standards talked about in this book to use in your life.

CHAPTER ONE
WHAT SELF-ESTEEM IS AND HOW IT DEVELOPS

Self-esteem is a general feeling of prosperity which emerges when we have healthy degrees of Self-Respect (liking our motivation), Self-Worth (liking ourselves), and Self-Confidence (liking our aptitudes). This feeling of prosperity which accompanies elevated levels of self-esteem is an uncommon encounter for a considerable lot of us. Maybe this feeling of prosperity is uncommon even among psychologists and possibly that is the reason we don't hear particularly about it.

Self-esteem is an expression that has come to mean many things. Here and there, confidence is a self-clear expression; however, it has likewise turned into a dubious idea with a wide range of implications. We realize self-esteem is critical to have, yet have likewise been instructed that it's conceivable to have an excessive amount of confidence. There are additionally numerous subsidiaries of confidence we talk about that may confound us when we attempt to characterize confidence; things such as self-worth, self-responsibility, self-confidence, self-love, self-assertiveness, self-acceptance, and self-assurance.

For our motivations, we will characterize self- esteem utilizing three of my preferred definitions:

- Self-esteem is the health of the brain.
- Self-esteem is the invulnerable arrangement of cognizance.
- Self-esteem is simply the reputation we have.

Much the same as the health of the body is an outcome or impact of many related causes, so it is with self-confidence. If we wish to build our wellbeing, we can just do as such by chipping away at it in a roundabout way by dealing with our eating regimen, our activity, our mentality, our condition. In this way, it is with self-esteem. In the event that we wish to expand our confidence, we can just do as such by chipping away at it by taking a shot at those things that add to it.

Much the same as a body with a weak immune system

is dependent upon the numerous germs in the earth and experiences the impacts of illness on a more regular and more serious level than a body with a strong immune system, so an individual with low self-esteem is liable to the "germs" of cognizance, for example, question, demoralization, judgment, evasion, refusal, and addictions.

Concerning the reputation similarity, to have a reputation with ourselves infers that there are various angles to us-there is the piece of us that thinks, feels, and acts, and there is the piece of us that "witnesses" or "judges" the thoughts, sentiments and conduct. This is basically valid; there is the self-image and there is the Spirit or Soul. You may likewise consider it "oneself" (lowercase s) and "Oneself" (uppercase S). The Self is simply the genuine; it is "God Within", our celestial nature and potential, our intrinsic undying being-what existed before our introduction to the world and will exist after our passing. Oneself is the physical or surface level sign that is brief in nature. It is the physical body, its reality is the five faculties and the feelings, contemplations and convictions that course through it. Both self and Self are significant pieces of what our identity is. Be that as it may, for this relationship, self-esteem can be viewed as the reputation oneself has with the Self.

Without a healthy self-esteem as an establishment, work done in some other zones of individual or profound development will eventually not last. If self-esteem is too weak, there won't be the fundamental inspiration to attempt to improve or develop by any stretch of the imagination. If we don't feel essentially commendable and meriting joy and development, regardless of what we do, we will figure out how to self-harm ourselves with the goal that our outer reality coordinates our inside truth of what we accept we merit. Much the same as we don't need to be in tip-top physical shape to start a program of activity, we don't need to have too healthy confidence to start a program of individual or profound development.

The Two Major Parts of Self-Esteem

There are two significant parts to confidence:

1) Self-Worth: feeling qualified to be glad

2) Self-Confidence: feeling positive about our capacity to think, adapt and adjust to life's difficulties.

We'll cover every one of these two significant parts differently, since they need to be well-understood. In any case, we can see that the two sides are significant; we should feel both commendable and ready to work in this life and to discover bliss and importance. They are cut out of the same cloth. Without feeling commendable, regardless of how capable we may think we will be, we will self-harm our advancement. Without feeling capable, regardless of how commendable we believe, we will linger and maintain a strategic distance from expected activity to achieve our development and we will feel overpowered by life and "stuck" as we watch life cruise us by. As we increment our view of our value, we additionally increment our impression of our capacity, and as we increment our capacity by taking on difficulties and conquering them, we likewise increment our view of our value. Along these lines, the different sides go about as either an upright cycle of upward energy into otherworldly and self-awareness or an endless loop of descending winding into gloom and stagnation. Simply realize that regardless of your present situation, you can turn it around - which is great and terrible news I assume. Yet, such is reality.

Is Self-Esteem a Natural Birth Right?

Some good-natured individuals throughout your life may have attempted to instruct you that self-esteem is a bequest, something we have just to guarantee by rehashing certifications or mantras. Others may accept that confidence is a blessing that guardians or others give youngsters by revealing to them the amount they are cherished and avowing how extraordinary they are. These convictions depend on misleading statements, and all things considered are non-beneficial.

While the facts demonstrate that we as a whole have inborn worth and boundless potential as offspring of God, that potential must be delivered from the domain of undiscovered potential to the domain of genuine reality through individual decisions. While the facts confirm that guardians and others can affect a youngster's confidence, confidence can't decisively be given to you by anybody but your Self - it must be earned and kept up through individual decisions.

Similarly, as the wellbeing of the body requires the structure squares of wellbeing great data sources and propensities as nourishment and exercise, so the health of the brain (self-esteem) requires the fundamental structure squares sketched out above. The correct utilization of cognizance isn't hard-wired in to us, it doesn't come consequently. Or maybe there are clashing inclinations of childishness (from oneself) and selflessness (from the Self) and the ever-present component of individual decision associated with singular obligation.

I see both a healthy body and a healthy personality as significant deep-rooted achievements against the ever-present powers of entropy (dis-request). Be that as it may, much the same as it is more earnestly to get from being flabby to being fit as a fiddle than it is to keep up being fit as a fiddle, so it is more enthusiastically to get from low confidence to high self-esteem than it is to keep up high self-esteem. This is the fundamental guideline of dormancy.

It's fascinating how the fundamental laws of material science apply to both the body and brain just as to our physical universe. As we'll see all through our whole adventure of otherworldly and self-awareness, the fundamental rules that oversee the regular world additionally administer the universe of our own bodies and brains. They are not simply comparable or appropriate; they are one and the equivalent.

What Does Healthy Self-Esteem Look Like?

Would you be able to see self-esteem? Truly, you can. Similarly as should be obvious whether a body is essentially healthy or fundamentally wiped out by taking a gander at it for indications of wellbeing or affliction that show themselves in the physical structure, so you can see whether an individual's self-esteem is essentially healthy or fundamentally wiped out by taking a gander at the physical signs of self-esteem.

Would You Be Able to Have Too Much Self-Esteem?

I don't think so. It would be like asking, "Would you be able to have an excess of good wellbeing?" You can have a lot of personality strength of Spirit or self-dominance of Self; however, as we've just clarified, that is really an indication of too minimal self-esteem, not all that much. In the event that we comprehend self-esteem to be the health of the brain, we see that wellbeing is about appropriate parity about being focused, grounded, appropriately working and in congruity. Limits on either side are undesirable.

Individuals with high self-esteem are not headed to make themselves look superior to others and they don't quantify themselves against others. Their happiness is in being what their identity is, not in being superior to another person. They listen first and when they talk it is with empathy and consolation.

How Self-Esteem Develops

There are two fundamental segments of healthy self-esteem: the feeling of individual worth and a feeling of individual capability or viability. These two segments of self-esteem develop over some undefined timeframe with numerous encounters.

The principal significant segment of self-esteem, the feeling of individual worth or being deserving of regard, ordinarily comes from being cherished or esteemed by others, regularly by guardians in the home. For instance, realizing that one's conduct and status truly matter to others enough to make them have genuine feeling and to incite activity from them adds to this sentiment of self-esteem.

The subsequent segment, a feeling of capability or adequacy, originates from the degree to which one considers oneself to be the reason for impacts. The pith of self-esteem is the inclination of affecting things and having the option to cause or influence occasions. Having calm trust in one's potential capacity to adapt to life's difficulties adds to sentiments of fitness.

By and large, self-esteem is seen as the result of assessing oneself against at least one criterion and arriving at anticipated norms on these criteria. These criteria regularly shift among societies and subcultures. In the United States, self-esteem is regularly founded on the assessment of oneself in six significant territories:

- One's acquired enrichments, including insight, physical qualities, and characteristic capacities;
- Feeling amiable and adorable;
- Being a one-of-a-kind human being, of significant worth, and deserving of regard;

- Feeling in charge or liable for one's life;
- Moral excellence or trustworthiness;
- What one has accomplished one's aptitudes, assets, and triumphs.

The overall criticalness of these zones changes with age and stages throughout everyday life; in this way, an individual's self-esteem isn't static or consistent all through life. For instance, youngsters ordinarily esteem sentiments of being amiable and adorable, esteeming the input got from guardians or other huge grown-ups. As they approach pre-adulthood their consideration starts to move from acknowledgment and input from grown-ups to the criticism got from their friends. For instance, young ladies right now regularly esteem their appearance and their reputation with their friends, while young men normally esteem their athletic ability and the acknowledgment they get from athletic challenge.

As people approach adulthood, the centrality of these elements starts to change and individuals become less reliant upon the criticism got from others. They start building up their own qualities, models, and desires. They assess themselves against their very own criteria and disguise the wellspring of self-esteem. For the most part, the feeling of uprightness, how much they feel responsible for their lives, and the level of accomplishment they have accomplished at the objectives they set for themselves take on more noteworthiness.

There is typically a characteristic move from reliance upon outer wellsprings of criticism from others to more disguised wellsprings of self-esteem as one sensibly assesses oneself against one's qualities. At the point when grown-ups keep on depending essentially upon outside wellsprings of criticism from others, it has been named "pseudo self-esteem," for healthy self-esteem of grown-ups depends on sensible assessment of one's self in connection to inward sources.

The degree of self-esteem is ordinarily generally stable at a specific stage throughout everyday life; however, it might be influenced marginally as one takes on new difficulties and encounters achievement or disappointment simultaneously. At the point when one's self-esteem is generally founded on inward sources, one is substantially more liable to have a steady degree of self-esteem than those people who are profoundly needy upon outer sources and the criticism from others.

The degree of one's self-esteem can likewise fluctuate as one sets better standard for oneself or endeavours to achieve something of essentialness. In these occurrences, one's degree of self-esteem can be influenced by the result of one's conduct and the level of accomplishment. This current one's degree of self-esteem can likewise impact observations about self-ability.

Self-esteem additionally vacillates as one experiences different phases of adulthood, as one looks for a profession, as one's kids grow up and leave, as one methodologies likewise changes as one experiences different phases of adulthood, as one looks for a vocation, as one envisions the time of retirement, or as one resigns. Every one of these advances can cause significant dangers to one's self-esteem since one is changing the essential premise whereupon one's self-esteem has depended. This is the reason being laid off from work, or having one's kids venture out from home can bring about huge drops in one's degree of self-esteem and can prompt gloom.

Another reason for the vacillations in one's self-esteem has to do with the individual assessments that are made by contrasting one's abilities and characteristics and proper companions. This has been named the "social correlation" hypothesis of self-esteem. This records for the way that numerous mentally talented kids show generally low self-esteem when put in programs with other skilled understudies. They may have contrasted themselves positively and others in a heterogeneous homeroom, yet when put with a select populace of other talented youngsters their self-esteem may endure.

Healthy self-esteem doesn't happen unintentionally or as a blessing. It must be developed, must be earned. It can't be achieved by being showered with acclaim, nor by material acquisitions, nor without anyone else's input talk, nor by being given ridiculous information. What has been discovered as of late is that one individual can't give another self-esteem. Guardians, educators and coaches can be effective by making the conditions that empower youngsters to develop in their capacities and figure out how to utilize their self-premise whereupon one's self-esteem has depended.

Self-esteem can develop, just as you grow a physical muscle. It needs practice and reiteration. At the point when you go to the rec centre and exercise, you do it consistently and over and over, until one day you will see the distinction in the physical state of your body. This is the equivalent for building up any passionate/character ability. Just here you practice mental/enthusiastic exercise rather than physical exercise, yet the outcomes are the equivalent.

Self-esteem is tied in with tolerating ourselves despite any inadequacies and disappointments. It is a psychological decision. It is essential to understand the advantages of advancing healthy confidence that lead to mental prosperity, assertiveness and versatility.

It merits rehashing the way that your own thoughts maybe have the greatest effect on your self-esteem, and these considerations are inside your control.

The ABCs of Self-Esteem

The ABCs of Self-Esteem require your trustworthiness, an open glad heart, and love of yourself when working through the ABCs, and it will lead you to phenomenal change in your self-esteem and mental self-portrait.

Is it accurate to say that you are prepared to raise your self-esteem? Here we go...

Accepting yourself initially is the quickest and least demanding approach to tolerating others. Acting naturally aware of your frailties will lead you to pass judgment on others for something very similar. It's a characteristic response. Work on tolerating yourself first and tolerating others will be a breeze.

Believe in yourself. That is the thing that guides, tutors, and we holistic mentors confer upon you. We move and rouse you to cultivate your normal qualities and to use those characteristics, to arrive at your maximum capacity. We see those characteristics in you. You have to trust you have them in you, as well.

Creativity is the stamp of legitimacy. Everybody has one. Being inventive is about substantially more than just craftsmanship. It's your own touch to inventive arrangements. How you set up things together. It's interfacing the majority of the specks that originate from motivation to deliver something exceptional - paying little respect to what it is. Utilize your creative mind. Be unique. Communicate and be inventively you.

Determined. Ever see that individuals who sparkle brilliant, stand tall, and are loaded with certainty are additionally decided? In case you're not resolved to move in the direction of something that increases a mind-blowing value, you're most likely burning through a great deal of time wishing you did. Quit sitting around, get decided and pursue your desire.

Eye-to-eye connection builds healthy connections, the benevolence you need. Looking enables you to share your contemplations, feelings, and perspective. It sets up genuine associations and builds trust with others. In case you're awkward when looking, centre both of your eyes around their one eye. Push through the uneasiness. The reward, a genuine association.

Focus. Interruptions are all over the place, you can't escape them, particularly not from frailty. Weakness takes your consideration and childishly utilizes everything up. The most ideal approach to keep centred is to be an eyewitness in your life. Simply see what's going on before you consistently. Take it all in. Take in the sights and scents. Watch how others communicate with each other. Tune in to how they address one another. Also, when you do lose your concentration to cynicism, simply remember it. Recognize that it's simply your negative self-talk, and return to concentrating on what's going on before you.

Gratitude builds your idealism, energy, and generally speaking prosperity. At the end of the day, appreciation makes you feel better. Attempt it! Pause for a minute to glance around at your environment. Look past the materialistic things; search for the straightforward things that life offers. Take a gander at the magnificence in nature. The air we relax. Thoroughly consider the previous 24 hours for minutes when you were thankful. Notice your vitality change.

Happiness is an attitude, not an ultimate objective. Rehearsing appreciation is just a single method for arriving at the condition of joy. Another approach to accomplish satisfaction is by bouncing all over on the spot for 30 seconds. Do it now. You'll see a moment change in your mentality as you feel for bliss.

Independence is a definitive objective. Regardless of what culture, race, religion, nation you were conceived in, each individual, even you, is striving to go after freedom. Be straightforward with yourself. Create self-trust. Act naturally dependent and enable your own contemplations to pass judgment on your encounters. It will lead you to act naturally roused and to your maximum capacity. Anything less, and you risk depending on others for approval, stripping you of your freedom and self-esteem.

Joy. It's in all that you do. If you can't discover it, this is on the grounds that you have a desire for what it ought to be. Relinquish your assumptions; that is not what happiness is. Fall into anything that you're doing. Lose all sense of direction at the time and let euphoria fold over you.

Kindness, and self-empathy. Utilize delicate language with yourself. Sooth and solace your spirit when something unkind occurs. Practice mindfulness to get your negative self-talk and supplant it with self-sympathy. You're human. Give yourself authorization to be one.

Love yourself genuinely. Try not to lament qualities you never had. Take a gander at the ones you do have and value them. Investigate the mirror and recognize them. Thusly, it changes your physiology and it will make you sparkle so brilliant that others will need a few.

Mindfulness - acknowledge what can't be changed. Make space among you and your considerations as though you're watching yourself, and enable your contemplations to go without judgment. Mindfulness is a condition of being that decreases pressure and nervousness, and lets you simply be.

Nurture your own needs. At last, satisfying them is your obligation. Anticipating that somebody should fulfil your needs puts you on a way to feeling unfilled. Simply recall, everybody is searching for something very similar. Would two be able to individuals searching for very similar things fulfil each other's needs? By fulfilling your own needs, it leaves you with some extra to save.

Open your psyche. Gain some new useful knowledge. Don't simply consider new ideas; break out of them by and large. The world is loaded with circumstances standing by to be gotten. In any case, if you live inside your usual range of familiarity, too hesitant to even think about making botches, you'll always be unable to go after them.

Here's something I frequently share with clients: "Our most noteworthy interests lie on untraveled territory." Don't accept you won't appreciate something until you attempt it. Open your brain. The open doors are unending.

Patience is a righteousness and an absolute necessity. The best things in life accompany time. Tolerance and duty toward your self-awareness will lead you to arriving at your maximum capacity.

"**Q**uality not Quantity," that is my saying. Do you centre around the measure of qualities, abilities, and endowments you have or on the quality and profundity of them. It's a bogus supposition to think the more qualities you have, the happier you will be. Take the 2-3 of your conspicuous qualities and make them astounding.

Resilience accompanies point of view. The point of view you have of yourself and of life. It's difficult to be flexible in the event that you don't confide in yourself, underestimate your blessings, and think inadequately about your capacities. Try to think about your achievements and your commitment to it. Do only that, and next time life tosses you a curveball you will feel enabled and versatile to beat it.

Sincerity. Be genuine. There's nothing more terrible than returning home toward the day's end feeling like a deceiver. It makes it difficult to investigate the mirror knowing you're a cheat. Talk from the heart, live by your qualities, and let your realness control you.

Tenacity gets you to the end goal. It energizes you with positive feelings and brilliant compliments. It supports your certainty and self-esteem higher than ever. Tenacity is a trait you as of now have. You should simply turn it on by making a pledge to yourself to take whatever you start to the end goal - every single time, regardless of whether the result is an apparent disappointment.

Unusual is equivalent to unique. Giving yourself authorization to be uncommon (unique) enables you to open up and act naturally. Huge numbers of us are so worried to fit in we become scared of our inventiveness. Give your genuineness a chance to manage you in your decisions and simply be you. You will, in a split second, notice a softness inside your heart and skip in your progression.

Vivid means strikingly brilliant or extreme and loaded with life. Self-esteem is based on your decision of how to approach and live. Everybody has zones throughout their life that can without much of a stretch be striking (e.g., family, vocation, otherworldly practices, side interests, and so on). Start seeing the striking quality in your life and watch the brilliance and power spread all through.

Wonder. Live with amazement. It intends to watch, see, and welcome encounters into your existence with a soul of miracle. It intends to free yourself of your assessment, judgment, and inclinations and to enable a feeling of miracle to shape your life. It intends to permit euphoria, bliss, and supernatural occurrences to be a piece of what your identity is.

Xuberant. The spelling is off base. I know. I did it deliberately. At times, being at the time and EXCITED about existence likewise means disrupting the guidelines (not all that much, obviously). I did it since it adds ZEST to The ABCs of Self-Esteem. So, by obtaining the letter “e” from "overflowing" to make another word "Energy" for no rhyme nor reason other than to show that it is so natural to add immediacy to life, regardless of whether it has neither rhyme nor reason. In addition, there isn't a word that starts with "x" that fits the spot. So, it's a slippery method to continue working the ABCs without forgetting about a letter. So!! Since you now know why I did it, did it put a grin all over? Be straightforward. Choose at this moment, for no rhyme nor reason, to be extravagant.

Youthful on a fundamental level, what an excellent spot to be. It's a sheer indication of immaculateness. An unadulterated heart is free from the majority of the negative impacts in our reality. You may be thinking about whether it is even conceivable to accomplish that. Furthermore, I state, YES, it is workable for you, and for everybody to accomplish. If you simply invest more energy concentrating on yourself and less time concentrating on every other person, being youthful on a fundamental level will be inside reach.

Zest is the thing that you add to life when you apply the ABCs to self-esteem.

There you have it, The ABCs of Self-Esteem. Appreciate the journey...

Measuring Your Self-Esteem

Self-esteem may show up as an elusive trait; however, there are procedures accessible to gauge its power!

➢ Rosenberg Self-Esteem Scale

Rosenberg self-esteem scale is a famous device to quantify confidence. It is generally utilized in sociology research.

Read the statements and rate them on a size of 0 to 3 as indicated by your consent to them. In the event that the total is below 15, you have to deal with improving and expanding your confidence.

- Strongly agree→ 3
- Agree→ 2
- Disagree→ 1
- Strongly disagree→ 0

Statements	Strongly Agree	Agree	Disagree	Strongly Disagree
I have great characteristics.				
I believe I am a whole lot of nothing.				
I feel pointless now at times.				
I wish I had progressive confidence.				
I feel like a disappointment some of the time.				
I have an upboosting demeanour.				
I am fulfilled throughout everyday life.				
I am not glad for myself.				
I get things done just as anybody can.				

So, today, take a couple of minutes to audit the table of what healthy self-esteem is all about, just this time, be mercifully legitimate with yourself. Have your Self be simply the mentor. Ask yourself the above questions.

The objective here is mindfulness, not flawlessness or taking care of every one of our issues simply being increasingly mindful of how undesirable self-esteem will in general appear in our lives - so we can see it when it's going on as opposed to being oblivious in regards to it. This mindfulness is a basic initial step, since we can't improve what we don't think needs improving. Then again, we may be very much mindful of our unfortunate self-esteem. In the event that that is the situation, the objective isn't to give the self a chance to disparage and put down itself significantly more, but to acknowledge what it is currently and realize that it doesn't need to remain as such, and by taking on the different practices that add to healthy self-esteem, we can and will improve our self-esteem.

For me, when my self-esteem gets "wiped out"- when the health of my mind weakens, I tend more towards the burdensome side. I contrast myself adversely with others I believe are achieving more than I am. I see individuals my age or more youthful that I see have a greater amount of something than I do and I can begin getting down on myself. At the point when I do get acclaim, I will in general reduce it or not recognize it as genuine. "No, extremely, it's not all that, I'm only a beginner." I likewise will in general abstain from looking for input from others, or standing up to issues head on.

Everybody is somewhat unique, and we as a whole have work to do to improve the health of our mind. Once more, the significant thing at this stage is to turn out to be progressively mindful, increasingly aware of how we display side effects of "wiped-out" self-esteem. At that point we can see it when it's going on and make a stride back and watch it happen - perceiving the truth about it. From this situation of expanded separation, or expanded seeing, we can start to take care of business, rather than just indiscriminately responding and not monitoring what's truly going on.

CHAPTER TWO
CAUSES OF LOW SELF-ESTEEM

The reasons for low self-esteem can be difficult to distinguish; there is no single cause for everybody, and a few people languish over an assortment of reasons. In any case, coming up next are some basic circumstances that factor into self-esteem, and getting acquainted with them can assist you with recognizing probably a portion of the causes throughout your life.

Uninvolved/Negligent Parents.

Much of the time, and especially when we're youthful, our emotions about ourselves are intensely impacted by how others feel about and treat us – particularly our folks or gatekeepers. Everybody merits a caring family, yet some youngsters have the hardship of not getting satisfactory help at home. Guardians or gatekeepers with emotional well-being issues, substance misuse issues or different difficulties will be unable to furnish their youngsters with the consideration, direction and consideration they need and merit. This can cause critical self-esteem issues for youngsters, as the individuals who should think about them most may not appear to.

Negative Peers.

Similarly, as the manner in which we're treated by parents or guardians can incredibly impact our self-esteem, so can the manner in which we're treated by peers. Being a piece of a social gathering that cuts you down – by not regarding you, by constraining you to accomplish things you're not happy with, by not esteeming your thoughts and emotions, and so forth – can make you feel like something isn't right with you, or that the main path for you to be loved is to do what others need and not tune in to your own heart and brain. This is harming to how you see yourself.

Trauma.

Abuse – regardless of whether physical, passionate, sexual or a blend of these – frequently causes sentiments of disgrace and even blame. An individual may feel that the person in question planned something to merit the maltreatment, that the person was not deserving of the regard, love and care of the abuser. Individuals who have endured abuse may have a lot of tension and misery related with the occasion too, which can meddle with an individual's capacity to lead a satisfying life.

Body Image.

Body image is an enormous factor in youngsters' self-esteem, particularly that of young ladies. From the minute we're conceived, we're encompassed by ridiculous pictures of what ladies ought to resemble, what the "perfect" body type is. Ladies' bodies are always generalized in the media, causing it to appear just as their bodies exist for others to see, contact, use, and so forth. At the point when pubescence comes around and our bodies begin to transform, they don't change into what we see on magazine covers or in music recordings. This can prompt inclination, ugly and insufficient, over the significant debilitation that accompanies considering yourself as an article for others to observe.

While young ladies are excessively influenced by body-image messages, young men aren't insusceptible. Numerous youngsters battle with low self-esteem related with pressure and body organization – especially concerning bulkiness.

Small Fish, Big Pond.

It's simple for youngsters to feel gobbled up in a world outside their ability to control. This prompts sentiments of inadequacy, feebleness and uselessness. In spite of the fact that the vast majority don't encounter it until adulthood, it's feasible for youngsters to experience the scandalous "existential emergency" – when doubt is raised concerning a significant issue. *What am I doing here? How do I make a difference?* A failure to respond to these inquiries can represent a critical test for one's feeling of self-esteem.

Unreasonable Goals.

Regardless of whether the pressure originates from them, authority figures or friends, some youngsters expect an excessive amount of themselves as far as school accomplishment, extracurricular association as well as economic wellbeing. The individuals who battle scholastically may figure they ought to get straight A's constantly; the individuals who perform well scholastically may attempt to take on an excessive number of different exercises and hope to be "the best" at all of them. Youngsters who long for prevalence may anticipate that everybody should like them – something that basically doesn't occur, in light of the fact that, regardless of what your identity is, it's not possible to satisfy everybody. The inescapable inability to meet ridiculous objectives may prompt the inclination that you are a disappointment when all is said and done.

Past Bad Choices.

At times we get secured in a specific example of basic leadership and acting. Maybe you haven't been an awesome companion previously. Possibly you didn't put forth a concentrated effort in school. Possibly you took an interest in dangerous practices like drug use or unprotected sex. You may believe you're only "the sort of individual" who carries on in those ways. You may even avert yourself essentially in light of past decisions; however, don't figure you can change courses now. Thusly, you won't attempt. You'll keep settling on decisions that fortify your very own negative self-see.

Negative Thought Patterns.

At the point when you become accustomed to feeling, contemplating yourself with a specific goal in mind, it progresses toward becoming propensity. You've most likely known about muscle memory – when you've played out a specific physical action like riding a bicycle again and again, your cerebrum consequently flags your muscles to do whatever that action requires – keeping you adjusted on the seat, for instance. Your contemplations and emotions really work similarly at times. If you have regularly felt that you're useless or sub-par, in the event that you always think negative contemplations and criticize yourself, at that point you're probably going to continue feeling and thinking a similar way except if you break the cycle by testing your negative considerations and sentiments about yourself. Similarly, as our muscle memory can become familiar with the incorrect method to play out a physical action, our idea and feeling recollections can learn based on examples.

The above eight reasons for low self-esteem aren't the main ones, but they're genuinely normal. The last one – the advancement of pessimistic idea designs – might be answerable for the perseverance of low self-esteem in the vast majority, paying little respect to the underlying causes. Youngsters ought to look at circumstances in their lives – at home, in school, social circles, for instance –

just as their very own dispositions and considerations – about their bodies, objectives, past decisions and feeling of direction, for instance – to recognize potential wellsprings of low self-esteem.

CHAPTER THREE
HOW TO BUILD SELF-ESTEEM

Relatively few individuals know about how much effect low self-esteem can have on an individual's life. Having low self-esteem can significantly diminish a mind-blowing nature all in all - it can prevent you from building healthy and cheerful connections; it can deny you of a stable and satisfying vocation and can put you in danger of creating conduct and psychological instabilities. I for one have encountered a portion of these results; actually, they were what caused me to choose to search for an approach to improve my self-esteem.

I don't think there is anybody in this world who might need to have low self-esteem. Tragically, however, the variables that summoned to shape this intense subject matter is frequently outside our ability to control. Fortunately, we have authority over what we do with the self-esteem that we have. You can either sulk with your low self-esteem for your entire life or choose to take a shot at improving it. In any case, you should remember that improving your self-esteem would require some serious energy and would require exertion and commitment.

Step-by-step instructions to build self-esteem is a question numerous individual consider. Tragically, the one thing that can have the greatest effect in our lives is a subject that is not taught in school. That is the reason a considerable lot of us battle with this idea long after we arrive at adulthood. We long to act naturally guaranteed and sure; however, we're never given the apparatuses to get it going.

It doesn't need to be that way. You can turn into the individual you've constantly longed to be. Also, you can begin at the present time. The key to building enduring trust in yourself is to concentrate on your convictions. (Furthermore, fortunately, it's not as hard as you might suspect.)

Our convictions influence each part of our life. They're the reason for our contemplations, our activities, and our degree of self-esteem. As Benjamin Franklin said, "If you think you can, you can. And if you think you can't, you can't."

How you see yourself and your capacities will decide an amazing nature. For example, if you accept you're not deserving of progress, you'll avoid openings that present themselves, and damage your endeavours. The equivalent is valid in your own life. If you don't feel you merit the affection and profound respect of somebody unique, you'll wind up pulling in the inverse; somebody who treats you the manner in which you internally feel about yourself.

The outcome of these sorts of activities is that you believe you have "verification" of your insufficiency and an explanation behind your low self-esteem. It's an endless loop that can proceed inconclusively. The way to halting the cycle, is figuring out how to build self-esteem and handling these convictions at their very centre. You need to decimate the restricting convictions keeping you down, and build up an engaging new belief system.

The trouble ordinarily lies in getting to these covered convictions. They're regularly intuitive. The key is to not overthink the procedure and enable your mind to bring them out normally. To do this, you basically should be separated from everyone else with your considerations incidentally, something that in this quick-paced world doesn't occur all the time. However, it's in these peaceful minutes alone where genuine knowledge can happen.

For example, have you at any point seen that you frequently get the best thoughts when you're in the shower? Or on the other hand felt totally invigorated and clear on what you have to do in the wake of going for a stroll in the forested areas? This is on the grounds that these are the few spots where you're in reality alone with your thoughts.

You can begin revealing your shrouded convictions by presenting a greater amount of these intelligent minutes into your life. It doesn't need to be a tedious procedure either. A couple of minutes of reflection every day can prompt stunning changes in your contemplations and convictions.

You can achieve this through contemplation, journaling, or doing practices which are explicitly intended to uncover these convictions and tell you the best way to build self-esteem. For example, pick one of these subjects to consider while alone with your considerations: Love, Success, Money, Relationships, Courage, Power, Career, Self-esteem. Consider how you truly feel about the word, about what it really means to you.

One lady did this activity with the word "self-esteem," since she reliably battled with low self-esteem. She was astonished at the considerations that abruptly sprang into her head after a couple of snapshots of calm reflection: pompous, arrogant, smarty pants, flaunt. She understood that despite the fact that she'd been attempting to build her certainty for quite a long time, she'd furtively been subverting her very own endeavours because of the negative convictions she had encompassing certainty.

When your actual convictions are revealed, you can then just make and strengthen a lot of engaging convictions to supplant the constraining ones from quite a while ago. This should be possible through attestations, and remaining mindful of your contemplations to guarantee the old convictions don't return crawling into your head.

As somebody once stated, "It's not who you are that keeps you down. It who you believe you're definitely not." How to build self-esteem is extremely a procedure of connecting with your convictions, and guaranteeing you have positive, engaging ones that push you ahead.

Here's a fundamental actuality that I presume you know effectively: “Great self-esteem is the way to accomplishment.” Regardless of if it is connections, professions, public activity, account - anything, you will consistently require great self-esteem. So how would we build self-esteem?

How about we see it like an issue.

1 - Characterize the issue.

2 - Consider it.

3 - Take a look at the solution.

4 - Set up the solution. Simple! (Well, I realize it isn't that simple, but how about we work thusly.)

1. **Characterize the issue** - When it boils down to it, self-esteem is as a rule about contrasting yourself as well as other people. We as a whole intentionally or subliminally arrange individuals, we appreciate and admire a few people, we disregard or speak

condescendingly to other people, (loathsome yet evident); it's about how we see ourselves in connection to other individuals - we rationally give ourselves a characteristic of how we remain in the public eye. At the point when you have low self-esteem, you believe everybody is superior

This is on the grounds that you have a bogus perspective on yourself and that is the stub of the issue. For what reason is it a bogus view? This is on the grounds that you have put a bogus incentive on yourself when contrasting yourself with others; you are too self-basic.

2. **Consider it** - First, we should utilize a similarity. Low self-esteem is just as you've put an off-base value ticket on something in a shop window. Suppose that you and your partners at work were the things in the shop. All of you do or produce something very similar, all of you get paid comparatively, yet the shop chief has put $100 sticker price on them and $1 on you, all of you accomplish something very similar, he's clearly made a mistake.....and think about who is the administrator liable for putting an inappropriate value ticket in a thing in a shop - that is correct it's you, since it's you who deals with

your life. Along these lines, you're the person who can address it, you can put the correct sticker price on by expanding the value; for example, you increment or build your self-esteem.

Second, self-esteem isn't something that is in your qualities, you regularly observe siblings and sisters with very differentiating characters, it's something that is very close to home to people. Fortunately, how to build or increase self-esteem is something that can be learned. Fascinating fact, did you realize that as per studies, around 60% of us have low self-esteem? Along these lines, you're certainly not the only one.

3. **Take a look at the solutions** - In order to realize how to build self-esteem, you need some self-examination to get a genuine target perspective on yourself. We as a whole have qualities and shortcomings, record them, when we recognize them, we have our base to expand on. What are you great at? What do you like doing? What might you want to be great at? What do you do gravely? What don't you like doing?

Next, characterize what's essential to you. Try not to think compliments from individuals from the opposite sex or your boss exceptionally significant. It may feel better; however, it won't be lasting. Concentrate on greater things. The vast majority of us need a glad and satisfying life, we need to acknowledge and outperform our potential, accomplish things - think thusly.

Presently, everybody is extraordinary; however, in order to build your self-esteem you should acknowledge that you should change. Nothing unique will happen except if you do.

Here's an expansive rundown: see it, add to if you need, select the ones that are fitting to you, be straightforward and take a gander at your rundown of qualities and shortcomings and perceive how they apply.

Self-Respect - Stop thrashing yourself, kill all self-analysis.

- Attitude - Bad things occur, be sure, centre around the solution not the issue. Treat any failure as an exercise, not a mishap.
- Relationships - Blend with positive, not negative, individuals.
- Social aptitudes - Try to be quiet, kind,

gracious and have great habits. Regard and tune in to other individuals and comprehend their needs.

- Review your own propensities.
- Embrace change - don't fear it or be negative.
- Share, co-work and impart

4. Set up the solution - Focus on building up the above aptitudes, focus on them. Be resolved in viewpoint - this is generally significant.

Envision being fruitful in your activity, socially or seeing someone but have the correct qualities. Representation is an amazing asset frequently utilized by elite athletics individuals, so it will assist your assurance with building self-esteem.

In the event that you figure out how to build your self-esteem, it will set you onto the correct way, you will find that you become increasingly effective at work, socially and seeing someone. In the event that you have poor self-esteem, it resembles a descending winding prompting despondency and blocking you in accomplishing anything - so don't surrender, be resolved.

Why It's So Important to Build Self-Esteem.

The basic reason for a ton of despondency is low self-esteem (an absence of trust in your very own value or capacities). Self-esteem is an incredible result history, qualities and condition. Low self-esteem is typically combined with weakness and self-doubt. These negative parts of "oneself" have an awful propensity for causing self-damage and diminishing certainty.

It's appalling to observe how low self-esteem incapacitates one's life through dread and uncertainty. The cruellest piece of low self-esteem is that regardless of how healthy your conviction is about the amount you trust you merit something, low self-esteem will figure out how to destroy any odds of achievement except if you oversee or mend it.

We should take a gander at the model seeing someone. It's a powerful urge for a great many people to draw in and keep up a cherishing, steady and fun close accomplice. At the point when the relationship is yet to show, the longing strengthens until the universe pleasantly plans to put you at the correct spot at the perfect time to frame this potential association. In the event that your self-esteem is moderate to high you will act naturally, show your best characteristics and enable the relationship to develop naturally. In any case, if your self-esteem is low you will freeze at the smallest recognition your potential accomplice has lost intrigue, act in manners conflicting with your actual qualities and penance substantially more of yourself than is proper so as to support a relationship that where it counts you don't trust you really merit.

So also, with regards to changing your vocation way, if you don't have a high self-esteem you will tarry, settle on poor choices and abstain from going for broke because of an exceptionally high dread of disappointment.

How you feel about yourself legitimately impacts on your life achievement and, generally speaking, bliss.

CHAPTER FOUR

HOW TO IMPROVE SELF-ESTEEM

Self-esteem is made out of the beliefs, emotions, and thoughts we hold about ourselves. Since our considerations, sentiments, and convictions change constantly, our self-esteem is additionally continually developing. Having low self-esteem can negatively affect your psychological well-being, connections, and school or professional life. In this manner, before you set out on any life change, it's basic that you first work on improving your self-esteem.

While there are transient convenient solution answers for improving your self-esteem, it ordinarily sets aside a touch of effort to, right off the bat, locate the hidden reasons for low self-esteem and afterward to start to expand your self-esteem and self-assurance utilizing an assortment of methods.

While it can require some investment to completely build self-esteem, an extraordinary method to start boosting self-esteem is through approval (inward and outside). This implies recognizing and respecting the commendation you get by others and setting aside the effort to normally give yourself acclaim for each and every activity very much done - rather than simply excluding it as another activity to tick off your plan for the day. These could be as basic as lauding yourself for:

- going to an occasion that made you feel apprehensive
- posting a profile on a dating site
- finishing an overwhelming introduction
- reaching somebody you really like
- shouting out about something you feel firmly about
- going after that incredible position
- contributing your cash
- cleaning your home
- taking care of your tabs on schedule
- making time to think about a friend or family member
- investing energy with a companion from abroad or interstate

Every day you do a horde of awesome things that you either overlook or make light of just on the grounds that they are not as significant as the errands you have chosen are most critical to lead you towards accomplishing your long-haul objectives. While these assignments are incredible proportions of achievement, setting aside some effort to recognize the various extraordinary things you're doing day by day will expand your self-esteem. Thus, it will expand your trust in your capacity to make your bigger wants a reality.

Thus, acclaim yourself as well as other people routinely and be glad for all the magnificent things you accomplish for yourself as well as other people every day. Be that as it may, there are various approaches to rest easy thinking about yourself and boost your self-esteem.

➢ Increasing Your Self-Esteem

Be purposeful with your beliefs and thoughts. Attempt to concentrate on positive, empowering, and valuable contemplations. Keep in mind that you are an extraordinary, exceptional individual that merits love and regard - from others and from yourself. Attempt these techniques: Use cheerful explanations. Be hopeful and maintain a strategic distance from the inevitable outcome of negativity. In the event that you anticipate terrible things, they frequently happen. For instance, in the event that you envision an introduction going ineffectively, it could possibly. Rather, be certain. Let yourself know, "Despite the fact that it will be a test, I can deal with this introduction."

- Focus on "can" and keep away from "should" statements. "Should" articulations infer that there is something you should do and this may make you feel compelled if you can't meet these desires. Rather, centre around what you CAN do.

- Focus on the positive. Consider the great pieces of your life. Help yourself to remember things that have gone well as of late. Consider the abilities you've used to adapt to testing circumstances.

- Be your own cheerer. Give yourself positive support and kudos for the positive things you do. Give yourself kudos for rolling out positive improvements. For instance, "My introduction probably wouldn't have been flawless; however, my partners posed inquiries and stayed connected with — which implies that I achieved my objective."

Set goals and desires. Make a list of things you need to achieve and decide to accomplish these objectives. For instance, you may choose to volunteer more, take up another leisure activity, or invest energy with companions.

- Make sure your goals and desires are practical. Making progress toward the unthinkable will just empty, not improve, self-esteem. For instance, don't all of a sudden choose that at age 40 your fantasy is to play proficient hockey. This is unreasonable and your self-esteem will probably endure a shot once you understand the distance away and unattainable that objective is.
- Instead, set increasingly sensible objectives, such as choosing to figure out how to play the guitar or another game. Defining objectives

that you can deliberately progress in the direction of, and in the long run meet, can assist you with halting the cycle of negative reasoning that leads to low self-esteem. At the point when you set and meet objectives effectively, you will feel a feeling of satisfaction and increasingly ready to relinquish your sentiments of low self-esteem for not meeting optimistic and generally unattainable life objectives, such as being the ideal sweetheart or immaculate cook or impeccable whatever.

- You could likewise set goals that help you see and feel your own skills. For instance, if you have a feeling that you need to be better educated about the world, conclude that you are going to peruse a paper each day for a month. Or then again, state you need to enable yourself in realizing how to fix your own bicycle and pick to figure out how to do your own check-up. Meeting objectives that address things that assist you with feeling amazing and able will assist you with resting, easy thinking about yourself in general.

Take care of yourself. A few of us invest a lot of energy agonizing and thinking about others that we disregard our very own physical and mental prosperity. Then again, a few of us feel so terrible about ourselves that we believe it's inconsequential to place time and exertion into thinking about ourselves. Eventually, dealing with yourself can likewise help improve your self-esteem. The more beneficial you are at the top of the priority list and body, the better the likelihood that you will be happy with yourself. Note that dealing with yourself doesn't imply that you must be thin, overly fit, and faultless. Rather, it means giving a valiant effort to be healthy, whatever that may look like for you exclusively. A few pointers include:

- Eat at any rate three suppers per day that depend on healthy and supplement rich nourishments, for example, entire grains, poultry and fish, and new vegetables to keep yourself invigorated and fed. Drink water to hydrate your body.

- Avoid sugary and stimulated drinks. These can

influence your disposition and ought to be maintained a strategic distance from in case you're worried about emotional episodes or negative feelings.

- Exercise. Research has demonstrated that exercise can give a genuine boost to self-esteem. This is on the grounds that exercise makes the body discharge the "cheerful synthetic substances" called endorphins. This sentiment of happiness can be joined by expanded inspiration and vitality. Attempt to get up to at any rate 30 minutes of overwhelming activity in any event three times each week. In any event, put in a safe spot time for a lively walk each day.

- Reduce stress. Make an arrangement to lessen the pressure of your regular daily existence by assigning time for unwinding and exercises that bring you delight. Think, take a yoga class, garden, or do whatever action makes you feel quiet and positive. Note that being focused can once in a while make it simpler for individuals to blow up or let negative emotions rule.

Think back on your life and your achievements. Odds are that you are not giving yourself enough kudos for everything that you've done for an incredible duration. Intrigue yourself, not others. Set aside some effort to reflect and glance back at your past wonders from enormous too little; this won't just assist you with ending up progressively mindful of these achievements but can likewise help approve your place on the planet and the worth you bring to the individuals and society around you.

- Grab a note pad or diary and set a clock for 20-30 minutes. During this time, compose a rundown of the majority of your achievements. Remember that everything ought to be incorporated, from huge achievements to the little ordinary things. Your rundown can incorporate things like figuring out how to drive, attending a university, moving into your own loft, making an extraordinary companion, cooking an extravagant supper, getting a degree or recognition, getting your first "grown-up" work, etc. The potential outcomes are huge! Come back to the rundown intermittently to add to it. You'll see that you have parcels to be pleased with.

- Scan through old photographs, scrap books, yearbooks, trip tokens, or much think about making a composition of your life and achievements to date.

Accomplish things you appreciate. Put aside time to accomplish something that fulfils you consistently, regardless of whether that implies cooking, perusing, working out, planting, or going through an hour simply chatting with your life partner. Try not to feel remorseful for this time you've put aside to appreciate; you merit it. Rehash that announcement as required.

- Experiment with new exercises; you may find out about abilities or aptitudes you didn't know you have. Perhaps you take up running track and find that you are great at long-separation running, something you'd never thought of. This can help increment your self-esteem.

- Consider taking up aesthetic exercises, for example, painting, music, verse, and move. Imaginative undertakings regularly assist individuals with figuring out how to communicate and accomplish a feeling of "authority" of a subject or ability. Loads of network sentences offer free or sensibly estimated classes.

Help somebody. Research has indicated that individuals who volunteer will in general feel more joyful and have higher self-esteem. It might appear to be incomprehensible that to rest easy thinking about yourself you should help another person, yet the science does without a doubt that sentiments of social connectedness that go with volunteering or helping other people make us feel increasingly positive about ourselves.

There are unlimited chances to help other people on the planet. Volunteer at a retirement home or a destitute sanctuary. Engage with your congregation in a service to the wiped-out or poor people. Give your time and administration to an others conscious creature cover. Be a Big Brother or Big Sister. Tidy up a neighbourhood park on a network sorted-out event.

Adjust your self-image as required. You change constantly, and you have to refresh your impression of yourself to coordinate your present self. For instance, expanding your self-esteem is silly if the picture you hold of yourself isn't exact. Possibly as a child you were extremely healthy in math but now you can scarcely compute the zone of your home. Possibly you were once profoundly strict; however, now, you recognize freethinker and never again go to chapel. Alter your impression of yourself to coordinate with the substances of your present life. Try not to anticipate that you should be extraordinary at math or to have some connection to otherworldliness.

- Evaluate yourself dependent on the NOW and your present aptitudes, interests, and convictions, and not on some past form of yourself.

Relinquish the idea of flawlessness. No one is flawless. Make that your new mantra. You're never going to have the ideal life, the ideal body, the ideal family, the ideal occupation, etc. Neither will any other person.

Flawlessness is a counterfeit thought made and multiplied by society and the media and it does an incredible insult to a large portion of us by recommending that flawlessness IS achievable and the issue is essentially that we're unsatisfactory.

- Focus on exertion as opposed to the longing for flawlessness. If you haven't taken a stab at something, you're apprehensive you won't do it flawlessly; at that point, you don't stand an opportunity in any case. In the event that you never go for the b-ball group it's an assurance that you won't make the group. Try not to let the strain to be impeccable keep you down.

- Accept that you are an individual and that people are in a general sense blemished and commit errors. Perhaps you talked too cruelly to your youngster or lied at work. It's alright. Individuals commit errors. Rather than criticizing yourself for your mistakes, see them as chances to learn and develop and as things that you can redress later on. Possibly you'll understand that you have to think all the more cautiously before you talk or that lying is never something to be thankful for to depend on. Excuse yourself and push ahead; this isn't simple; however, it's a vital aspect for maintaining a strategic distance from that cycle of self-indulgence and low self-esteem.

➢ Dealing with Low Self-Esteem

Discover the triggers of your low self-esteem. Consider any disturbing conditions or circumstances that may be identified with why you feel bad about yourself. For some individuals, regular triggers may incorporate work gatherings, school introductions, relational issues at work or home, and huge life changes, for example, venturing out from home, evolving employments, or isolating from an accomplice.

- You may likewise need to consider individuals who make you feel bad about yourself. You can't control any other person's conduct; what you can control is the manner by which you react and how you let their conduct sway you. If someone else is treacherously inconsiderate, mean, or pretentious or insolent towards you, comprehend that he may have his own issues or intense subject matters that is making him act adversely towards you. In any case, if this individual is setting off your low self-esteem, it is ideal if you can leave or expel yourself from circumstances where that individual is available, especially if they react adversely if you attempt to face him about his conduct.

- While other individuals' conclusions and thoughts have their place in your life, don't set your life as per them. Tune in and accept what works for you. You are the legislative leader of your own life. Nobody else can do that for you.

Know about the thought patterns that wear down your self-esteem. For a ton of us, negative considerations and convictions can turn out to be ordinary to such an extent that we simply expect them to be exact impressions of the real world. Attempt to know about some key examples of reasoning that damage your self-esteem:

- Turning positives into negatives - You rebate your accomplishments and positive encounters. For instance, in the event that you get an advancement, rather than considering it to be a reward for your diligent work, you reduce your moral obligation: "I just got the advancement on the grounds that the supervisor lives in my neighbourhood."

- All-or-nothing or paired speculation - In your brain, life and all that you do just has two ways. Things are either fortunate or unfortunate, positive or negative, and so forth. For instance, if you don't get in to your top school but get into five others, despite everything you conclude that you're a complete disappointment and useless in light of the fact that you didn't get into Harvard. You consider things to be either all great or all awful.

- Mental sifting - You see just the negative side of things and channel out everything else. This normally brings about contortions of people and circumstances. For instance, if you made a grammatical error on a report, you accept that the report is presently useless and that your supervisor is going to believe you're moronic and not capable.

- Jumping to negative ends - You expect the most noticeable awfulness when there is no proof to help that conflict. For instance, "My companion didn't react to the welcome I simply sent a half hour back, so she should despise me."
- Mistaking affections for realities - You conclude that how you feel is part of a bigger truth. For instance, "I feel like a complete disappointment, so I should be an absolute disappointment."
- Negative self-talk - You converse with yourself in negative terms, including put-downs, ridiculing, and self-deploring humour. For instance, in case you're five minutes late, you chide yourself more than once and call yourself "moronic."

Make a stride once more from your thoughts to revaluate them. Rehash these negative considerations to the point that they become foolish or as though another person is stating the words. Consider how if you rehash a similar word again and again it starts to separate (have a go at doing this with "fork" for a model).

Such activities can assist you with getting some good ways from your thoughts so you can watch them with more noteworthy objectivity, practically like you are an outside onlooker. You will likewise observe that these negative and foolish considerations are extremely just words, that's it. What's more, words can be changed.

Acknowledge the majority of your thoughts —even the negative ones! Despite the fact that the familiar maxim is regularly to change or oppose certain negative considerations and emotions, this can, in certain cases, just exacerbate your poor self-esteem as you understand this is actually quite difficult. Rather, acknowledge these contemplations without essentially approving them. Negative considerations come into your head. They exist. They may not be correct; however, they do exist. You don't need to like them; however, you do need to acknowledge that you're having those considerations.

- Instead of attempting to control negative thoughts, try to reduce the power they hold over you. Understand that negative thoughts are counterproductive and do whatever it takes not to let them on a very basic level influence how you feel about yourself or your incentive on the planet.

Pair negative thoughts with positive contemplations. Change the negative things you consider yourself into positives.

For instance, if you reveal to yourself you are terrible, you could disclose to yourself that you look pleasant today. If you reveal to yourself you never do anything right, disclose to yourself that you accomplish loads of things right and give some particular models. Consider doing this activity in a diary to monitor your positive contemplations. Peruse them before you hit the sack and when you get up.

Make signs on post-it notes with these positive explanations and put them where you can see them, for example, on the washroom reflect. This can help fortify these announcements and instil them in your brain. Ideally, after some time, the positive thoughts will supersede the negative ones.

Stop comparing. Comparing ourselves as well as other people quite often brings about lower self-esteem. Your companion won a grant and you didn't. Your sister found a new line of work right out of being a student and you didn't. An associate has 500 Facebook companions and you just have 200. The more you contrast yourself with others, the more you are going to feel just as you come up excessively short. These examinations are out of line, not least since they expect every circumstance is equivalent.

Perhaps your sister found a new line of work actually rapidly on the grounds that she did a practical program with heaps of openings. Or on the other hand perhaps your associate has such a large number of "companions" since he will include pretty much anybody he meets. Remember, in addition, that you don't have the foggiest idea about the intricate details of any other individual's life but your own. Without a doubt, your companion may have a grant; however, perhaps his folks can't stand to support him and he works 20 hours per week at low maintenance over school.

- What you should concentrate on is yourself.

Contend with yourself. Challenge yourself to be better. Keep in mind, the main conduct you can control is your own, so that's what you should concentrate on.

CHAPTER FIVE

GREAT HABITS TO RAISE YOUR SELF-ESTEEM

Issues with self-esteem can make you feel like a disappointment or like you are shameful of consideration. Every individual, notwithstanding, has great characteristics and capacities that ought to be esteemed. If you are attempting to build up your self-esteem, there are healthy moves you can make so as to begin boosting your certainty. By additionally building up an upboosting mentality, you will be well on your way to a progressively guaranteed self.

➢ Building Up a Positive Lifestyle

Look after yourself. Raising your self-esteem most importantly means saving time and consideration for yourself. Demonstrating that you esteem yourself is an initial phase in figuring out how to perceive how others esteem you. Ensure that you accomplish things like:

- Get a lot of exercise.

- Develop an everyday schedule for yourself that makes you feel better, for example, washing up toward the day's end or taking a stroll toward the evening.

- Gain another aptitude or pastime, build up an ability, or simply find out about subjects that intrigue you.

- Feel great about where you live! Put aside time to clean and embellish your home, even in basic ways.

Practice good eating habits. To feel better, you should be well-fed. This implies eating a fair diet. A few supplements, for example, nutrient D and nutrient B12, can even give your temperament an extra boost.

- Good wellsprings of nutrient D include: salmon, dairy items, and braced juices.

- Good wellsprings of nutrient B12 include: liver, invigorated oats, and dairy items.

Take time to do things you enjoy. Low self-esteem can cause a lot of pressure. In the event that you put in a safe spot time for things that you like doing, in any case, you can calm a portion of this pressure and interface with your feeling of self-esteem. Peruse a book, utilize a melodic or creative ability, go out to see the films or a game, invest energy with companions—whatever you appreciate!

Take time to do things you enjoy. Issues with self-esteem are regularly attached to emotions that you are fruitless. A decent cure for this inclination is defining and meeting an objective of achieving something. Indeed, even little achievements will make you feel progressively sure and effective.

- Doing things to improve the appearance and solace of your home can be an extraordinary spot to begin: cleaning your home, getting out a storage room, finishing, and so forth.
- Taking care of low pressure, low stakes assignments like getting things done or setting off to the market can likewise make you like achieving something.
- You can likewise focus on achieving long-haul

objectives, for example, bringing down or disposing of obligation, learning another work, getting in shape, and so on.

Dress well. While picture ought not be your essential inspiration, considering your appearance can positively affect your self-esteem. This doesn't imply that you have to purchase costly garments, nonetheless. Dress in whatever apparel you have that makes you feel sure, and your internal inclination will extend outwards!

Give yourself rewards. You can show that you esteem yourself if you let yourself have something exceptional now and, at that point. Giving yourself a reward shows that you care about all that you do, particularly if the reward comes in the wake of taking a stab at something.

- Rewards don't need to appear as material things. You can likewise compensate yourself with encounters. For example, you could go to a show in the wake of finishing a major undertaking at work or school.

Invest energy with great individuals. If you need to

help your self-esteem, at that point encircle yourself with individuals who are sure, strong, and kind. Keep away from individuals who are negative, mean to you, or appear to keep you down.

Practice kindness. If you are battling with liking yourself, take a stab at accomplishing something decent for another person. You will feel great that you bailed somebody out. Indicating that you care about others likewise helps your desires that others should think about you. Attempt:

- Practicing irregular demonstrations of thoughtfulness, for example, paying for a more interesting supper.
- Visiting a companion or relative who is wiped out.
- Helping neighbours with yard work.
- Volunteering for good aims in your locale.

➢ Recognizing Your Good Qualities

Make positive records. Setting aside effort to

consider positive parts of your life can be a moment boost to your self-esteem. By encircling yourself with great thoughts, you will drive pessimism crazy. Have a go at making arrangements of:

- Things you are grateful for
- Your great characteristics, (for example, consideration, persistence, and attentiveness)
- Strengths or gifts you may have, (for example, a great hard-working attitude, knowledge, imaginative or melodic capacities, aptitudes in a scholastic or expert region, and so on.)

Attempt a common complimentary exercise. Plunk down with a companion, relative, or another person you trust. Alternate offering each other compliments or depicting great characteristics that the other individual has. This basic exercise will help your own self-esteem and the other person's.

Keep a "positive scrapbook." Make an accumulation of things that commend you and your great characteristics. These might incorporate photos, letters, grants, gifts of spots you have been, and different tokens of positive things throughout your life. Make a point to add to continue adding to it, and look it over when you have an inclination that your self-esteem needs a boost.

- This doesn't need to appear as a real scrapbook. Any sort of gathering will do, for example, a container or show rack.

Make a self-esteem schedule. Take a schedule, and for every day, plan a little thing you can improve. These can incorporate things like: "Make my preferred dinner," "Call my companion," or "Take a stroll in the recreation centre." Check off the things you achieve every day, and consider how you feel thereafter.

CHAPTER SIX
WAYS TO MAINTAIN HEALTHY SELF-ESTEEM

Regardless of whether our degree of self-esteem is excessively low or excessively high, there are sure procedures that may assist us with counterbalancing any of these two boundaries and thusly we can restore the internal harmony. The normal hazard is subjectivity that can lead us to a misrepresented self-assurance or the other route cycle, an exceptionally low self-esteem. It is exceptionally prescribed to control our feelings and activities and to reassess from time to time the manner in which we respond when we are presented to specific conditions. Along these lines we grow step by step our very own target approach conduct. Mindfulness is unquestionably the key since we remain objective.

3 Major Reasons for Maintaining Self-Esteem

Each and every presence on the planet is recognized by its worth. Simply envision anything and its value shows up in your psyche before you see or have it. In like manner, you as a person are said to be something the size of your self-esteem. Your self-esteem is in actuality a sort of appearance of the picture you imagine in the reflection of your idea of self-comprehension. Do you genuinely think about how individuals take you? Does it truly make a difference about what casing individuals will in general fit you in? Perhaps your answer is indeed, you are in good shape. If you state "no", at that point you positively have three essential motivations to understand the significance of self-esteem and you must plan something to look after it.

1. Do Not Deny Your Own Worth

Denying your very own value implies you repudiate the estimation of others. You can't purchase something worth one hundred dollars against a bit of paper, which bears no worth. Neither would you be able to sell something of zero an incentive against a hundred dollar note.

Your very own genuine acknowledgment reputation and self-esteem gives you the privilege to get regard and respect of a similar worth that you feel is yours. So also, a healthy sign of self-esteem legitimizes your incentive to others for what they expect consequently.

2. Self-Esteem Boosts Self-Self-Esteem

The vitality transmitting from the heater of self-esteem is exceptionally amazing. It powers your fearlessness that thusly drives you forward in the general public and towards your fate of an effective life.

Self-esteem boosts up your energy on the track of accomplishing your objectives. It labels you with a specific worth according to other people and their conduct relies upon their comprehension and acknowledgment of your self-esteem. The more you show it the higher your cost is set in the bazaar social standing and individual connections.

3. You Are Bound to Acknowledge God's Blessings

Acknowledgment of self-esteem is an incredible gift of The Greatest Creator. Denying it suggests renunciation of further celestial endowments throughout everyday life, which no person can manage. You can't wage a war against God and get away without paying the cost.

Denying self-esteem makes you contemptible of any worth. It is much the same as discrediting your reality.

Indeed, even the littlest molecule of a particle has some worth that makes it worth essentialness. Amplify your value through your self-esteem.

Suggestions on Maintaining Self-Esteem in Various Situations

Attempting to keep up healthy self-esteem isn't as simple to accomplish as beating other ailments. It is a regularly perceived factor that in the event that we become unwell with a physical sickness, at that point we are slanted to trust in somebody, be it a companion or individual from family. Sadly, if the issue is of a psychological sort, we will in general be less imminent with conversing with individuals about the issue. Feeling down because of low self-esteem can be seen as an indication of shortcoming which is an uncalled-for suspicion. Battling with healthy self-esteem issues can transpire paying little respect to how rationally intense they may show up.

One stage that you should take when you understand you have an issue is to converse with somebody, ideally a specialist or an expert to keep you from being overpowered by low emotions. If you are taking on an excess of duty at work or worry at home, this may prompt things jumping over you. To keep up a healthy self-esteem you may need to take a rude awakening to guarantee that you are not over-burdening yourself with an excessive amount of going-on in your life. If you take up additional exercises to involve yourself, take up a side interest or game that will build your enthusiastic quality.

The key to remaining responsible for yourself and your objectives is to keep up balance in your life. Parity implies that you control the majority of the critical pieces of your life guaranteeing that they are attempting to together. Everybody's impression of parity is distinctive on the grounds that individuals' needs fluctuate contingent upon their individual needs throughout everyday life. You may have a more drawn-out working day than most on the grounds that it gives you the money-related prizes you have to suit your picked way of life.

Anyway, while you feel adjusted, this may not be the situation for other individuals. Their needs in life could well be extraordinary. Be that as it may in the event that you are feeling somewhat out of parity the smallest thing could influence your healthy self-esteem and be the beginning of issues.

At the point when you are a youthful grown-up, equalization might be accomplished through social exercises; however, as you get more established, secured business may turn into a need. In the event that you have turned out to be monetarily secured, you might need to rediscover yourself. Invest significant energy to take a gander at where you are and where you need to be, and think cautiously to keep up equalization and healthiness. Being content with your life is significant for keeping up healthy self-esteem.

Numerous individuals make suspicions of what is required to be mollified throughout everyday life. A portion of these suppositions are driven by social pressures, relatives, work associates and even the broad communications. The main concern is just you recognize what is best for you. Consider what is happening in your life; is it excessively rushed, are close relatives enduring because of, for instance, a too substantial remaining task at hand?

In a perfect world, what might you need to do?

Attempt to institute a procedure that will enable you to draw near to your objective. Parity in your life ought to never be disparaged. Your personal satisfaction will be unfathomably improved if you get the equalization right. Make sure to keep up healthy self-esteem; get help when it is required in light of the fact that you deserve it.

What really motivates you?

List five things that you want to get done but dearth the motivation to do

1	
2	

3	
4	
5	

What might the reward be for accomplishing these five things listed above?

1	
2	
3	
4	
5	

Maintaining High Self-Esteem in Harsh Environments

We realize that self-esteem is fundamental with the end goal for us to make extraordinary outcomes or progress throughout everyday life. Nonetheless, how can one keep up self-esteem when looked with harsh and predicament at work or at home? Are there individuals in your work environment or home causing you extraordinary misery, collapsing your self-esteem, hindering your objectives or execution? How can one stay brave during such tempests? Is it proper to say that you are ready to remain, cool, without a care in the world and when confronting these fierce waves?

Throughout everyday life, different circumstances and individuals come into our life as tests to our self-esteem. Envision yourself as an objective board and envision the circumstances and individuals that are making you extraordinary pain be bolts. These bolts will pulverize your self-esteem and force you down from numerous points of view. Don't allow them to decimate you, or defeat you. How can we manage such bolts throughout our life?

Here are a few hints you might need to consider as a manual for maintaining your self-esteem in when faced with these sharp bolts.

1. Negative Workplace

Is there a "merciless" circumstance going on in your working environment in which everybody is mostly worried about stretching out beyond each other at one another's cost? Such conditions are unfortunate and do nothing worth mentioning to one's self-esteem. Healthy challenge is basic for quality, improvement and achievement. Put forth a valiant effort to maintain a strategic distance from such conditions while advising yourself that it is your activities and reaction that decides your prosperity.

2. Negative Behaviour from Others

Tattle mongers, double-crossers and individuals who love cutting others down exist as a reality throughout everyday life. Acknowledge this reality while maintaining a strategic distance from these individuals as much as you can. Continually keep up your concentration and course. At the point when you are clear and centred around achieving explicit outcomes throughout your life, the pessimism that originates from these individuals will be debilitated and rendered feeble. Concentrate on finishing your particular errands and objectives, not yielding till you have accomplished them.

3. Changes in Our Life and Environment

Changes are unavoidable and imperative to advance throughout everyday life. This is a reality. View such changes in life as venturing stones to improve, rethink, and refine ourselves. Changes in life are frequently awkward and here and there unpleasant; however, we have two options in which to react. Reject them with fear and stagnate, or acknowledge them as a fundamental procedure for personal development and extension.

4. Past Experiences

Has somebody or a circumstance in life disturbed you? It is cool to say that you are as yet influenced by these past encounters, having hard feelings of resentment or hatred? Or maybe you had a past disappointment that you continue practicing in your psyche, unfit to look forward or move out of it. Gain from an earlier time; however, don't harp on it. Amassing an excessive amount of awful past is undesirable. Utilize the past as venturing stones to direct you forward, seeing disappointments or mishaps from your psyche as expectations to learn and adapt.

Throughout everyday life, we may in some cases

waver when hard times arise. A few people accept that you should be one of the "fortunate ones" who have been skilled by the sky with high self-esteem. Decide not to accept that! Keeping up high self-esteem, remaining and being sure is a decision. You can react to "awful" occasions throughout your life, by accusing destiny, conditions and other individuals. In any case, do such reactions serve you?

Just by reliably guaranteeing obligation regarding our contemplations, activities, words and deeds, would we be able to begin to grow genuine quality, assurance and self-control that exudes from our internal being? It is exceptionally prescribed to control our feelings and activities and to reassess from time to time the manner in which we respond when we are presented to specific conditions. Along these lines, we grow slowly our very own target approach conduct.

Mindfulness is certainly the key since we remain objective. Being adaptable is another procedure that can adjust the correct degree of self-esteem. Fixation and inspiration represent basic factors that keep up self-esteem. Act fearlessly regardless of the conditions, in light of the fact that expecting dangers is the most ideal approach to arrive at progress, and without fail, we experience achievement; we develop proficiently our self-esteem. Worth your qualities and concede your shortcoming. Life instructing has created numerous techniques dependent on this methodology of individual qualities and shortcomings and the significant advantages are noticeable on close to home and social plans.

This is the most ideal approach to guarantee and keep up high self-esteem consistently.

CHAPTER SEVEN
HOW TO HELP SOMEONE WITH LOW SELF-ESTEEM

Self-esteem, or the manner in which we feel about ourselves, is only one piece of our enthusiastic make-up. If you have high self-esteem, it might be hard for you to see a companion or a friend or family member experiencing low self-esteem. In spite of the fact that you can't make others rest easy thinking about themselves, you can offer help and consolation and model positive self-esteem.

➢ Offering Support

Be a decent companion. A decent companion can be useful by truly tuning in to the individual and addressing them from the heart. While it very well may be a test to keep up a companionship with somebody who is to some degree touchy, recollect this is (ideally) a brief state, and they are moving in the direction of progress.

- Make a push to invest energy with your companion. Individuals with low self-esteem frequently come up short on the activity to make arrangements with somebody. You may need to start plans yourself and stick with them. Trouble in connecting and finishing in social plans is certifiably not a slight towards you. Or maybe, it ponders the uneasiness, dread, or misery an individual with low self-esteem may have.
- Having a standard "date" can be useful. Regardless of whether this is a Sunday evening mug of espresso, Wednesday night poker night, or day-by-day morning swim, these occasions can be essential in helping you and your companion.
- Listen to your companion, looking while you are bantering. Converse with them about their issues, get some information about what's going on, and offer them backing and exhortation (but just when they request it). A touch of minding can go far. Indicating that

you care about your companion can help give them the help they have to improve their self-esteem.

Abstain from attempting to advise the individual how to think. You risk distancing the individual you are attempting to help if you legitimately disclose to them how they should consider themselves or how they should act. Rather, bolster your companion for what their identity is, and attempt to support them towards, and model, more beneficial enthusiastic self-care.

- If you attempt to counter the individual's pessimism, they may not react well. This isn't an issue comprehended exclusively by rationale.
- For example, if they state, "I feel so inept," it may not be useful to state, "No, you're not; no doubt about it." Your companion will probably effectively raise ways they are moronic - that is the thing that they have been thinking.
- Instead, take a stab at reacting to "I feel so

moronic" by saying something like, "I'm sorry you feel that way. What makes you imagine that? Accomplished something occur?" This can offer a road for a progressively beneficial discussion.

- Affirm their emotions. Simply having one's voice heard is engaging. It is enticing to attempt to contend that negative sentiments are ridiculous; however, you ought to dodge that.

Problem-solve, if the individual is capable. If an individual has low self-esteem, they may regularly customize the issue. The issue is with them, and it is something that appears impossible to be illuminated. It can have an individual come at it from a new edge. Keep in mind that critical thinking, more often than not, must be done after a portion of the more negative feeling is communicated.

Volunteer together. Helping someone else will in general boost self-esteem. By urging and supporting endeavours to help other people, you may support a companion's self-esteem simultaneously.

- Or take a stab at having them help you. An individual with low self-esteem incidentally will regularly be more ready to assist a companion than themselves. Offering a chance to enable another to can set up for a minute to accomplish something that builds self-esteem.
- For example, having an individual assist you with a relationship issue or fix your PC is useful.

Give a source of genuine sympathy. If your companion needs to discuss her sentiments or the foundation of their low self-esteem, the most accommodating thing you can do is tune in while they process these issues. Frequently, in the event that somebody distinguishes the underlying driver of their self-esteem issues, they understand that their negative sentiments about themselves originate from outside.

Propose inward voice adjustment. Ask your companion what their inward voice says to them about themselves. You'll likely find that their internal voice is continually negative. Attempt to instruct them to be progressively kind to themselves by halting the negative self-talk and turning it around to something positive.

Recommend therapy, tenderly, in the event that you figure it will be useful. If you feel that the other individual has further issues than you can by and by help with, have a go at recommending that they go to treatment. Both psychological social treatment and psychodynamic treatment can help with low self-esteem.

- You might need to approach this discussion cautiously. You would prefer not to estrange the other individual or make them feel that you think they are insane.
- If you have ever been to treatment yourself, clarify the amount it helped you before.
- Do not be shocked or upset if your recommendation is quickly dismissed. In the event that you planted a seed that will keep on developing in the other individual's psyche, they may in the long run choose to attempt a guide.

CHAPTER EIGHT
TIPS YOU CAN FOLLOW TO START CONQUERING SELF-DOUBT

Despite the fact that you'd most likely incline toward never questioning yourself until the end of time, self-doubt is an extremely helpful thing. It's a wellbeing system of the psyche that protects us by putting the brake on presumption, presumptuousness, or heedlessness.

All things considered, a lot of it tends to be unsafe, as it ends up upsetting, sincerely debilitating and incapacitating. Once in a while, self-doubt is the main thing that stands among you and the kind of life you need to lead. In the event that you ever feel as though you're at war with yourself, the accompanying tips will assist you with conquering your inner adversary, for the last time.

1. **Acknowledge It**

Self-doubt is a typical piece of the human condition,

so your initial step is to acknowledge that it's occurring - recall, the main individuals who never question themselves are mental cases! Urgently endeavouring to squash it down or disregard it just makes it more grounded. At the point when you can calmly inhale and state to yourself "alright, I feel dubious about this", you begin to unwind, opening up mental vitality.

2. Find the Patterns

As you figure out how to endure vulnerability, you'll have the option to see the sorts of circumstances where self-doubt will in general emerge. Ask yourself - "When, where and with whom do I feel most uncertain of myself?" Self-doubt is a propensity, not an element of your character. When you've distinguished the triggers for that propensity, ask yourself what's the littlest thing you could do to feel surer of yourself in that circumstance.

3. Put Aside a Doubt Time

Another helpful strategy for taking care of self-doubt is to save time for it to occur. Permit yourself ten minutes by the day's end when you will do nothing else with the exception of staying there and stressing over where you're turning out badly. If questions creep up on you during the day, record them, and guarantee yourself you'll obsess about them appropriately at the assigned time. This returns you healthily in charge.

4. Emotional ABCs

Doubt is a feeling, and feelings are powerless against reason. You can bring your legitimate, reasonable aptitudes to shoulder on self-doubt by following the ABC Model discussed above. Incomprehensibly, self-doubt is really a sureness - an assurance that you're off base or that you can't adapt. By utilizing the above strategies, you can give occasion to feel qualms about your own self-doubts, and land at an increasingly practical perspective on occasions.

Boost Confidence and Increase Your Self-Esteem with These Tips

Start your day out right by giving your self-esteem somewhat of a boost. Start every day by following these significant self-esteem starters:

- Play some vivacious (or unwinding) music to get you in the correct mindset for the afternoon.

- Smile! It'll make you feel good and look all the more engaging and appealing to everyone around you.
- Give compliments to yourself and everyone around you. At the point when you make another person feel much improved, you're probably going to feel better as well.
- Show some unconstrained fondness to your life partner, your children, even your pet. It's an incredible state-of-mind enhancer and giving a kiss and embrace can truly make you like yourself.
- Dress for progress. Nothing makes you have an inclination that you can vanquish the day more than dressing well. If you have an inclination that you have the right to wear that power suit, the chances are you'll have the certainty to utilize that capacity to further your potential benefit.
- Give yourself an energy talk. Take a couple of

minutes alone every morning to pick 2 or 3 things that you like about yourself. Possibly your hair looks particularly great toward the beginning of today or your jeans fit perfectly. Inform yourself so anyone can hear what's great regarding you that day. Furthermore, if there's a territory you have to take a shot at, reveal to yourself you can do it.

- Try something new consistently. Take a chomp of an obscure nourishment; stroll to work regardless of whether you don't figure you can make it; grin at an outsider. Give yourself the mental fortitude to have a go at something - anything - new each and every day.

- Say no at least twice before early afternoon. Disapprove of negotiability. Disapprove of tattle. Disapprove of the doughnut you'll lament eating. Figure out how to say no at any rate twice before lunch to whatever will sap you of your certainty and capacity to have self-esteem in yourself.

Your degree of self-esteem is the thing that decides

how you will figure, how you will act and how you will associate with yourself as well as other people all through the remainder of your day.

Set aside the effort to pursue the basic strides over every single morning to help support your certainty, help your self-esteem and start your outing in an increasingly positive and compensating way.

CHAPTER NINE

A FEW DIFFERENT WAYS TO BEGIN CARRYING ON WITH CONSCIOUS LIFE

To be progressively conscious and carry on with an increasingly conscious life, intend to know about yourself inside and remotely at every minute. In the event that you are cognizant, you know about the present minute and the way that your internal identity is stirred. It is being careful and feeling the air entering and leaving your lungs. It is being available with your thoughts and feelings.

A great many people don't live conscious lives. They live up in their minds with a lattice of contemplations whirling and spinning, and as a result of that they miss the "at the present time"; they don't encounter the totality of the wonderful present.

For instance, at a time you went on vacation and out of the blue, your impression of everything appears to be more noteworthy? You smell the outside air, grin at the lavish green trees and exquisite blossoms, and hear the sweet flying creatures singing. You feel increasingly invigorated and intermittently more joyful on the grounds that you have overlooked the many thoughts going around in your brain and you are essentially aware of the magnificence of your present environment. Those equivalent excellent environments could be in your neighbourhood back home, but you are centred around different things to see; you don't set aside some effort to smell your very own roses.

The most profound piece of what our identity is, our cognizance or soul, aches to be experienced. The issue is that it gets concealed by such a significant number of layers of negative things throughout the years. Youth wounds, negative emotions, constraining convictions, and so on heap on a seemingly endless amount of time and it gets increasingly hard to associate with our soul. To turn out to be progressively cognizant requires a stripping endlessly of these layers individually. The most suitable way to this is to end up careful or contemplate.

To carry on with a progressively conscious life, you're

expected to back off, get peaceful, and permit the agonizing injuries of the past to surface so you can process them and let them go; along these lines, burrowing down through layers to turn out to be more in line with your soul. As you do this, injuries recuperate and magnificence and completeness emerge. It is a lovely change.

You may be thinking, "Who needs to return to adolescence and face old injuries?" I comprehend where you are coming from, but it is a significant procedure in the event that you need to start carrying on with an increasingly cognizant life.

Consider these questions:

- Is it proper to opine that you are content with your life?
- Do you love what your identity is?
- Is it proper to opine that you are loaded with disgrace or agony?
- Do you know your main role throughout everyday life?

- Are your connections adequate?

If your responses to a portion of these questions are not what you'd like them to be, I welcome you to set aside some effort to dedicate to thinking every day. Figure out how to be available with your considerations and emotions in the now. Figure out how to sit peacefully and let your mind rest. Indeed, even only 10 minutes daily will be useful.

There are numerous approaches to contemplate; however, you need to plunk down in an agreeable position, take a couple of full breaths, and after that concentrate on your breath. As you continue breathing in, feel the air moving into your lungs. As you breathe out, feel the air leave your body and loosen up each muscle. As you centre around your breathing, in and out, every single other idea will soften away and you will feel settled. Irregular contemplations and sentiments, for example, old injuries, will surface once in a while and when they do, just recognize them and let them go.

Some call this procedure of ending up progressively conscious "illumination." The more edified you become, the more harmony, delight, and satisfaction you will feel. You won't lie in bed around evening time giving your considerations a chance to keep you conscious or fatigued during the day fixating on things.

Alongside reflection, you can carry on with an increasingly cognizant life every day by attempting to be careful and present for the duration of the day. Be aware of your ideal life and if contemplations must be there, be certain they are sure. Be aware of your environment. Hear the winged animals singing. Set aside effort to pat the feline. Sit outside and inhale profoundly the fragrance of nature. Grin frequently. Become mindful of breathing in and breathing out. Feel the centre of your being invigorated and well. Get to the base of what your identity is. You are substantially more than your fragile living creature and bones.

Think of carrying on with a progressively cognizant life, and as you do, you will find increasingly more what a great soul you are.

Benefits of Living a Conscious Life

There are times when I get only somewhat

downhearted and I end up asking, "Why carry on with a despondent life? What's the point?" I've seen this normally occurs during a specific, basic piece of the mending venture. The mending venture - the existence venture (they're synonymous you know) - has rhythms. There are sure, unsurprising examples that appear in our lives as mending happens. From a specific, two-dimensional point of view we can say - and everybody knows - that "life has its good and bad times." Those high points and low points are truly occurring on a three-dimensional level as an element of the development and compression of the Universe. Alongside this Universal swaying, Consciousness is growing and contracting. As a piece of the bigger Consciousness, our cognizance is growing and contracting, too.

It's the point at which I'm at the tightest piece of the compression, in the birth trench maybe, that I'm being approached to look all the more carefully at things that don't serve my true self. I'm being approached to get clearer on what I need and don't need, what works and doesn't work. I'm being approached to make some move for adjusting all the more totally with my bona fide self. Then again, it's the point at which I'm at the greatest piece of the extension that former connections are leaving to prepare for new ones. I'm finding that what I thought was strong isn't strong any more. There's nothing considerable to push off of. I'm being approached to give up. In either case, it appears that any place I place my consideration, it arrives on some adaptation of force and distress. It's during those occasions that I start saying, "What is the point? Why live intentionally?"

If we remain present, we'll have some degree of an immediate encounter of the very thing I just referenced, just as the knowledge that accompanies it: life grows and contracts. All things considered, it is and it isn't. On one hand it's remarkable on the grounds that it's the idea of Nature. Then again, it's additional customary, once more, since it's the idea of Nature. Regardless, if our being is only somewhat more associated with the normal, cadenced nature of life, whenever we experience the tightest piece of the constriction or the largest piece of the development, we'll be less well-suited to pay attention to our brain when it starts wishing things were the manner in which they used to be, or agonizing over where things are going. We'll be less adept to encounter the constriction and development of life as something that is smashing us and additionally tearing us separated. It often well may be progressively comparable to life is giving us a back rub; a little existential body work, maybe.

At the point when we add our cognizant thoughtfulness regarding life's rhythms; when we infiltrate the minute with a greater amount of our consideration, the bunches and the attachments - the protections - get worked out. We become a being all the more firmly lined up with the Source of life. We are orchestrated by Source. We entrain to Source - that is, the properties and qualities of Source are moved to us, legitimately, through reverberation. In our lives, the properties of Source uncover themselves as a real existence loaded up with four advantages: 1) a more profound feeling of fulfilment, 2) a more noteworthy degree of adequacy in all that we do, 3) a more prominent feeling of harmony and 4) more trust during the time spent life.

You may have encountered this in your conventional life and not really known it. You might have the option to recall when you were especially occupied with an action that is significant to you. You may recollect times when you were centred around that movement and times when you were progressively occupied. All things considered, the occasions where you were engaged stick out in your memory in light of the fact that there's a decent possibility that during the occasions when you were engaged, you saw the action as all the more fulfilling and you were most likely much better at it as well.

There are different conditions under which you may have encountered the impacts of profoundly infiltrating the present minute with your consideration. Perhaps you were truly debilitated. Possibly you were being hailed here and there. Perhaps you were suffocating. Or maybe you were amidst some kind of mishap. It's during these occasions that individuals report time backing off. They feel loose and tolerating of the circumstance despite the fact that serious damage or demise might be close within reach. It's during these occasions that individuals experience the tranquillity of associating with the Source and the trust that joins it.

Luckily, we don't need to sit tight for some dangerous occasion to transpire to have an encounter of infiltrating the present minute with more consideration. We can settle on the decision to carry on with a cognizant life. We can settle on the decision to focus on the present minute. The present minute wakes up: thoughts, feelings and sensations. At the point when we give the present minute our consideration, we see that these thoughts, feelings and sensations go back and forth; they extend and contract. The Universe is holographic in nature. That implies that the littler extensions and compressions of our faculties are visualizations of the bigger developments and withdrawals of the Universe.

At the point when we sharpen ourselves to the compressions and developments of our faculties, we are additionally sharpening ourselves to the bigger extensions and constrictions of the Universe. This implies through our faculties we can have an immediate encounter of the development and withdrawal of the Universe.

Once more, the advantages of this fourfold: an existence of 1) more profound fulfilment, 2) viability, 3) harmony and 4) trust.

CHAPTER TEN
HOW JOY AND SELF-ACKNOWLEDGMENT WORK TOGETHER

Opening up to Joy

To start to live in delight, you should adore and acknowledge yourself. What's more, in spite of the fact that I am not barring our higher presence, I am purposely concentrating on the littler self - the normal, human, regular you that should be cherished and acknowledged precisely all things considered, for how it has been, and for anyway it will be.

Acknowledgment is a component of self-esteem. Surrendering is its inverse and is an element of indifference. Aloofness shields us from encountering the delight inside us. Detachment is a distraction with the unaccepted and a decision made in the past. Capitulating to the surge of basic reasoning overpowers us and we ruminate on negative evaluations of the conditions, others, and ourselves.

"I can't control the breeze, yet I can control the sails."

Notice I said capitulating overpowers us, not the considerations. At the point when we become detached, we start to wind, descend, and we persuade ourselves that our circumstance is miserable and that the future will be the equivalent if not more regrettable than the past. We feel divided and feeble. Surrendering to this antagonism is simply the direct opposite affection and happy living. The experience of edification turns into a bad dream and something to escape, rather than a fantasy to be lived in.

"You truly need to cherish yourself to complete anything in this world." ¬Lucille Ball

Acknowledgment is different from apathy. Where surrendering renders us frail and keeps us stuck before, acknowledgment frees us from an earlier time and enables us to make positive move right now. Capitulating breeds dread. Acknowledgment is an opening to joy.

Our beliefs and thoughts frameworks influence us physiologically. The thoughts we think discharge synthetic substances into our framework. Negative thoughts exhaust us, and positive life avowing contemplations adjust us to our happiness.

You can't change the past; however, you can change your frame of mind towards it. Acknowledgment enables that change to happen. By moving ourselves to adore and acknowledge the pieces of ourselves that we may in the long run need to transform, we supersede the pundit that channels us, and we forbid the idea and conviction frameworks that exhaust our energy. Love and acknowledgment move us to make positive move.

What you have just done and thought is finished. Acknowledge what you have just done or not done, and move yourself from the past to the present. How you are with the present minute is what is important. It is a demonstration of shrewdness to adore and acknowledge your sense of self, your body, your contemplations, your emotions and your past. Start by adoring and tolerating whatever the condition you may end up in at some random minute.

Self-esteem is the most persuasive mending vitality. Self-esteem is the most noteworthy instructing and the one most routinely ignored. Its nonattendance keeps us dumb. We become stuck in a descending winding of making sense of everything. Endeavouring to seem clever in our discoveries, we become manikins of the modified inner self and captives to disappointment.

I propose that every morning, for the duration of the day, and again before resting, that you rehash to yourself, "Paying little respect to (what is or isn't going on, or has or has not occurred, or will or won't occur) I profoundly and totally love and acknowledge myself."

What's more, if you truly need to unravel yourself from the chains of the past, at that point you can stretch out the announcement to incorporate "others." "Paying little heed to (the thing someone or other said about me) or (my annoyance, or dread, or doubt about________), I profoundly and totally love and acknowledge myself as well as other people."

In the event that you are not prepared to incorporate "others" yet, then state, "Despite the fact that I am not prepared to incorporate others, I profoundly and totally love and acknowledge myself." Try it - it works.

Self-esteem is the best solution for inward confusion. Wishing and trusting that things were diverse alongside grumbling about what turned out badly is vitality exhausting to the point of disgrace, self-damage and physical disorder.

Positive sentiments can't exist together with negative considerations. Alter your perspective; change your state of mind.

Our bodies and our brains react in an open and positive way to life-improving information. Profound respect, appreciation, happiness, and diversion upgrade our gathering of progressively extended vibrations of our Life-force. The Life-force is actually that, a power of life. It is nurturing, and adjusts us to the delight of progressing interminable life. Every one of us is liable for encouraging the Life-force inside us and adjusting our psyches to get the most elevated levels of information. This is collaboration and subsequently co-making with Life.

(In the event that you are not in those encounters at the present time, at that point say, "Despite the fact that I am not feeling esteem, appreciation, merriment or delight, I profoundly and totally love and acknowledge myself.")

Then again, our bodies and our brains react contrarily to what has the goal of making us wrong. Normally, we do this to shield ourselves from pushing ahead. Self-damage is tied in with detesting ourselves to the point of not having any desire to be seen. Stowing away doesn't enable us to keep on being alive and prosperous. We stow away on the grounds that there are portions of our experience that we evaluate as disgraceful of acknowledgment and love.

(In the event that you play here a great deal, at that point say, "Despite the fact that I am stowing away and feel shameful of acknowledgment and love, I profoundly and totally love and acknowledge myself.")

Remember that we are here to develop and learn. We effectively overlook this when we become awkward with individuals and conditions in our lives. We overlook that the Universe in its unending shrewdness has designed these perfect conditions for our tutoring. This incorporates the individuals with whom we associate.

It is essential to recognize these reactions and the

conditions that apparently caused them.

"Despite the fact that I am angry with ___________, I profoundly and totally love and acknowledge myself."

"Despite the fact that I (did or didn't do such and such), I profoundly and totally love and acknowledge myself."

"Despite the fact that I messed this up, I profoundly and totally love and acknowledge myself."

"Indeed, even with these sentiments of self-loathing, I profoundly and totally love and acknowledge myself."

"Despite the fact that I am befuddled and lost in regards to ___________, I profoundly and totally love and acknowledge myself."

"Despite the fact that I thought I had this overseen, I profoundly and totally love and acknowledge myself."

"Despite the fact that I experience serious difficulties tolerating ___________ about myself (or another), I profoundly and totally love and acknowledge myself."

"Despite everything that has happened, I profoundly and totally love and acknowledge myself."

"In any event, when I don't comprehend what's going on or why, I profoundly and totally love and acknowledge myself as well as other people."

Since we are for the most part adapting, all of us are significant and required. We contact each other's lives in manners that may appear to be pointless and undesirable now and again and, in this way, we judge these connections as terrible or wrong. However, in a more noteworthy comprehension, everything is actually as it ought to be for the exercise and chance to extend and develop. This is the reason it is important to help ourselves to remember the fundamental standards of acknowledgment and self-esteem.

Joy is an element of tolerating what is. Self-esteem and joy go connected at the hip. Before change can be cultivated, acknowledgment of "what is" must happen. You can't change what you imagine doesn't exist.

It is hard to acknowledge the pieces of ourselves that we need to reject and abandon. It is likewise humiliating and once in a while embarrassing to perceive what requirements to change inside us in the event that we need to develop. By the by, we will develop. Furthermore, with the development comes change.

Enduring change consistently follows an internal change.

"To endeavour to change conditions before you change your imaginal (internal) movement is to battle against the very idea of things. There is no external change until there is an internal envisioned change." ¬Neville

A positive inward change harmonizes with the advancement of internal quality. Inward quality is an element of self-esteem. This internal quality (self-esteem) enables us to wind up mindful of what is really occurring within us, and outside in the outer universe of conditions. By recognizing and tolerating what's going on all around, we adjust ourselves to the activity of the omniscient, supreme and inescapable progression of affection. This is bliss. Harmony with this power is nurturing. Seen division from it, through renunciation and bigotry, is stifling.

Start to acknowledge yourself precisely as you are at the present time. It is a useful asset that opens us up to self-esteem.

Love changes. Love grasps. Love gives of itself. Also, in particular, Love never falls flat.

This is your life. Try not to miss it.

Self-Appreciation: The Key to Living a Joyful Life

How would you welcome yourself? Or then again, isn't that right? Did you discover that regarding yourself was narrow-minded? In the event that you said no, would you say you were terrible? If you adulated yourself or were applauded, were individuals apprehensive you may get a "big head?" The greater part of us gets the message boisterous and clear that applauding ourselves or others would prompt "getting to be prideful" or "relaxing." The awfulness of this conviction is that, truth be told, the exceptionally inverse is valid. What you focus on extends. Self-appreciation and valuation for others depends on affection and acknowledgment.

A lot of what we state and do is called "productive analysis." This implies I reveal to you something as far as anyone knows to "your benefit." What really happens is that I judge what you do and say dependent on "should" at that point I disclose to you how to "do it right."

At the end of the day, analysis is dangerous and leads individuals to sentiments of insufficiency: love and acknowledgment lead to sentiments of self-esteem. Keep in mind: the most significant errand you have is adoring and tolerating yourself.

What Is Self-Appreciation?

Self is characterized as the whole individual of an individual, while thankfulness is characterized as a judgment or assessment; a statement of profound respect, endorsement, or appreciation. Self-appreciation is tied in with saying: "I acknowledge myself precisely as I am." It is tied in with recognizing our extraordinary blessings and knowing inside every one of us is a profoundly innovative, gifted being simply hanging tight for revelation.

Self-appreciation isn't tied in with putting others down or thinking yourself better; it is tied in with cherishing ourselves the manner in which we are and thus adoring others the manner in which they are. Recollect that: I can possibly acknowledge and cherish you if I will adore and acknowledge myself and recognize my own self-esteem.

In the last investigation, as the Dalai Lama expresses, "The reason for our lives is to be cheerful." Happiness in my psyche compares with bliss. The delight, without which all other bliss is decreased, is happiness in one's self. Self-pride and self-happiness are as indispensable to the person as are air and water. Self-appreciation is the foundation in deciding one's wellbeing, one's prosperity, and one's bounty and flourishing in both our open and our private lives.

Practical Steps to Self-Appreciation

1. Pronounce your uniqueness. There will never be another you; another who is actually similar to you; another who will make a commitment to the planet in precisely the manner in which you do.

2. Search for the things you like about yourself. Record them and after that, focus on one thing daily, for example, “I am equipped,” “I am imaginative” or “I am presently making my optimal life.”

3. Forgive yourself. The past is finished; realize that you were doing as well as could be expected with your degree of information and comprehension around then.

4. Use confirmations to help yourself to remember your holiness. Put them on the refrigerator, mirrors, any place, to advise yourself that you are exceptional. For instance, "I like and welcome myself," "I am a loveable, important individual and merit the best life brings to the table."

5. Read books that rouse you. Books, for example, day-by-day reflections, considerations for the afternoon, adages and citations from moving pioneers set the pace for making a frame of mind of delight as well as harmony before you start your day.

6. Practice a "mentality of appreciation." We have made a lot to be grateful for, our wellbeing, our plenitude, and our opportunities. Convey a little scratch pad with you and record everything that you are appreciative for throughout the day. You will be stunned at all the endowments throughout your life - your companions, your family, your activity, your warm home, the way that you don't need to stress over stepping on landmines or

getting your head brushed off as you venture out an entryway.

7. Be consistent with yourself. Carry on with the existence you have imagined for yourself. Try not to seek others for endorsement; search inside, and you will think that it's everything.

CHAPTER ELEVEN
EMOTIONAL INTELLIGENCE AND HOW IT CAN HELP YOUR SELF-ESTEEM

Emotional intelligence (EQ) is tied in with monitoring your emotions. If you have a high enthusiastic knowledge you comprehend what you are feeling from minute to minute, and as a rule, you additionally know why you are feeling as you do. Moreover, you realize what it is that you have to do so as to change your feelings in circumstances when you wish to feel in an unexpected way. Emotional intelligence along these lines makes you progressively mindful of your own needs and it builds your capacity to take great consideration of yourself.

High emotional intelligence can't be unaccompanied by high awareness. In this way, if you have a high EQ you additionally realize yourself well. It is simpler to build a high self-esteem (for example, to build up a decent association with yourself) when you know yourself. How might you acknowledge and love somebody when you don't have a clue? Therefore, self-esteem and emotional intelligence go connected at the hip. As you raise your enthusiastic knowledge, you additionally figure out how to comprehend yourself better, acknowledge yourself (counting both pessimistic and positive feelings), fulfil your own needs and worth yourself more. Everything gets simpler when you improve the association with yourself.

Emotional intelligence isn't just about getting oneself, but additionally about understanding other individuals. With a high EQ, you can go into a room brimming with individuals and promptly get a feeling of how the individuals in that room are feeling right then and there. You can comprehend other individuals' needs better, and this makes it simpler for you to assist them with satisfying those necessities. This makes it simpler to deal with every single distinctive sort of individuals since you realize how to affect them greatly. We as a whole have a social need, and as we raise our emotional intelligence, we become better at building and keeping connections that assist us with fulfilling that need. We make ourselves feel much improved and we raise our self-esteem by helping other people feel better.

To raise your enthusiastic knowledge, you just need to hear yourself out more regularly. Enjoy a reprieve and ask your body what it is feeling. Do you feel some pressure or agony anyplace? Tune in to your instinct (your hunch). When you open up to the data that is as of now inside you, you will discover that you "know" significantly more than you knew about previously. Try not to disregard or attempt to push feelings away. They have something critical to let you know. Your feelings will assist you with raising your self-worth.

How to Develop Your Social Aptitude and Your Magnetism

You are going to find a lot of intuitive personality control methods and methodologies that have the ability to cut through any issue or obstruction you have throughout everyday life. For a large number of years, these procedures were known distinctly to spiritualists and alchemists.

Never again.

In the only remaining century, great books like *Think and Grow Rich,* and *The Power of Your Subconscious Mind* offered access to these old and life-changing insights to the general man or lady in the city. In this article you'll figure out how to apply them to making social progress, anyway that way to you.

Love, kinship, network regard. Everything is yours for the taking. You should simply tap your gigantic and interminable intuitive personality power.

Your subliminal personality is the genuine wizard behind the blind. At the point when you come into this world, you are prearranged with a couple of endurance components and learning impulses, but that is about it. As you develop and travel through the world, you gather data and structure convictions about how the world functions. If these convictions are engaging and life-attesting, at that point you are viewed as a "characteristic" and achievement is simple.

In any case, for most by far, constraining convictions are created, and fill in as a boundary to progress for some. Rather than seeing chance, we see deterrents. Rather than seeing achievement, we see disappointment. Rather than seeing things that can may make us feel better, we just spot things that may hurt us.

That changes today.

People are normally social creatures. We are at home with others. Our normal tendency is to coexist with others, share with others and make others giggle and grin and feel better. That normally appealing individual who goes into the room and blows some people's minds is living in their regular state.

Utilization of subliminal personality control.

Your intuitive personality should be retrained with some uniquely made attestations, that should be utilized with a certain goal in mind to expand the intensity of your subliminal personality.

The initial step is to make your certifications. Note them in the present, positive tense, as though they are now valid. Let's assume them as you are depicting your optimal social self. If you got on wish from an enchantment genie, how might you be? Depict that future you, in the current state.

Indisputably, the perfect time to rehash your mantra is that time just among cognizance and obviousness, just on this side of rest. This is the time that your subliminal is least impervious to changes, and will take on new thoughts the fastest. Go through five to ten minutes, a few times each day, rehashing your confirmations.

The best occasions are exactly when you wake up, and similarly as you nod off around evening time. If you can get into the act of really nodding off while murmuring your insistences to yourself, that will turbocharge your outcomes.

Keep this up for half a month, and watch the magic happen.

5 Ways to Unlock Your Social Potential

As you are reading this book, there is a high likelihood that you aren't a social butterfly; you aren't somebody who will stroll into a room of complete outsiders and make companions; you are the sort that will simply remain around until somebody you know comes around. You can anyway change this, you can turn into a social butterfly, you can move toward becoming somebody who is normally agreeable and has so a lot of allure that you will have the option to procure trust and backing of the individuals around you.

Being an extrovert isn't hard and the points of interest to it are extraordinary; you make a great deal of new companions; you can find out about various societies and you will be significantly more joyful in the event that you can talk straightforwardly to individuals.

In the event that you aren't an extrovert or simply hoping to improve your social abilities, at that point keep perusing this area for the personal growth answers for increment or open your social potential.

1. **Be authentic.**

Try not to take a stab at being the individual that makes terrible quips or accomplishes dumb things that they typically wouldn't simply stand out. Act naturally, individuals will like you for that (in addition, in case you're not yourself, you will get figured out sooner or later and look idiotic).

2. **Be the best listener that you can be.**

Regardless of whom you are conversing with or if you are in a gathering or separately, probably the best ability you can create is tuning in. Look and tune in to the individual and you will have the option to get things from what they are starting to make discussion on (you will be astonished at what number of individuals don't listen but simply consider something keen to state).

3. **Roar with laughter.**

By this I mean don't pay attention to things. If somebody ridicules you, chuckle or if somebody makes a quip (a great one), snicker. Somebody who has a decent comical inclination will have the option to draw in individuals to them like a magnet.

4. **Be sure.**

If you aren't certain, at that point chances are individuals will see straight through you. If you feel certain it will appear and when you are sure you can pull in numerous individuals.

5. **Do random demonstrations of kindness**.

By doing random demonstrations of kindness you will have the option to develop your character and character is something that keeps individuals conversing with you. Thus, if you demonstrate you have a pleasant character chances are you will draw in individuals in.

By following these straightforward tips, you can figure out how to improve your social capacity and you will figure out how to improve as an increasingly adorable individual.

Along these lines, go on, I challenge you – I twofold challenge you – to continue to get a sensible vision of the reward for accomplishing what you have to accomplish.

What would motivate you to achieve more?

Very few people are motivated by money. We are not "in love" with money; what motivates us is what money can do for us.

What truly motivates you?

List five things that you want to get done but lack the motivation to do

1	
2	
3	
4	
5	

What might the reward be for accomplishing these five things listed above?

1	
2	
3	
4	
5	

CHAPTER TWELVE
THE DIFFERENCES BETWEEN SELF-ESTEEM AND SELF-CONFIDENCE

Numerous individuals utilize the words "self-esteem" and "self-confidence" as though they were equivalent words. Self-esteem and self-confidence are extraordinary. Self-assurance is one piece of self-esteem. Self-esteem is simply the more extensive class.

Your self-esteem is simply based on how you view yourself. Having a high self-esteem implies you are OK with yourself and content with the individual you are. Those with high self-esteem will never feel deficient or mediocre compared to others as they are content with the individual they are.

Consequently, it is a lot more extensive than self-assurance, as your self-esteem is the entirety you get when you include every one of your impression of yourself as far as what you achieve, how you feel, how you're carrying on towards others, how others act towards you, what befalls you during your life, your body observation, etc.

Self-confidence implies certainty that you can effectively get things done. In the event that you are self-assured, you put stock in your capacity to achieve the things that you set out to do. You can have high trust in certain regions while having low trust in different regions. For instance, you may feel sure about your capacity to find real success at work, yet you need certainty with regards to building and keeping up profound and satisfying connections. Self-assurance is based around your trust in your capacities which is very isolated, albeit connected with, self-esteem. Self-assurance can likewise change in various circumstances. You may feel totally certain about your capacity to carry out your responsibility well - high self-confidence - but have no trust in your capacity to ice skate - low self-assurance.

Your degree of self-assurance influences how well you figure out how to achieve whatever it is that you're attempting to do. An individual who is sure that they will pass a meeting is significantly more prone to do as such than an individual who doesn't accept that they will have the option to do it. Self-assurance in this way influences your accomplishment in life in an extremely useful way.

Self-esteem normally has more extensive results than self-assurance. It influences your associations with other individuals, what sort of occasions and individuals that you pull in into your life, your emotional wellness, your physical wellbeing and significantly more. Indeed, self-esteem influences EVERYTHING. If you need to change anything in your life - regardless of whether it is a particular issue or if you need to improve in some territory - you need to begin by raising your self-esteem. You may figure out how to raise your self-esteem as a side-effect of taking a shot at something different, or you may need to concentrate on your self-esteem straightforwardly.

Presently, you might be thinking, "I have never ice-skated; obviously, I would have low trust around there." However, you can have certainty that you will put forth a valiant effort and adapt rapidly. Going ice-skating with this frame of mind makes it more probable that you will adapt rapidly, fortifying your positive self-assurance.

So how would they influence one another? Well, for the most part, if self-esteem is high so is self-confidence and the other way around. There are exemptions to this anyway, as somebody can depict extraordinary self-confidence as something else.

In the event that your self-esteem is high, your certainty will in general be high as you acknowledge your deficiencies, qualities shortcomings and act as needs be. You can be trash at painting, but understand that you can't be great at everything and keep up your high self-esteem.

Growing high self-confidence can raise our self-esteem. As you become progressively positive about your activities and accomplishments (regardless of how huge or little), you remember you are a skilled, capable individual and along these lines self-esteem is raised.

Self-esteem and self-confidence go connected at the hip, and for you to carry on with the best life you can, you should chip away at both. The two of them can improve rapidly, altogether and definitely in a little space of time, with only a little work.

CHAPTER THIRTEEN VALUABLE DESCRIPTIONS OF VARIOUS TYPES OF BODY LANGUAGE AND HOW THEY CAN BE USED IN DIFFERENT SITUATIONS

Body language, also called "non-verbal communication," is very important. The manner in which you impart through body language can decide your accomplishment in everything from connections to your vocation. Up to 93 percent of correspondence can be non-verbal. Giving nearer consideration to the messages you send through body language can enable you to succeed.

People tend to speak with one another. This can occur in evident and in not all that undeniable manners. We talk, we compose. In any case, we can likewise convey without utilizing words by any means. If words are utilized to convey content, this nonverbal communication talks about our connections. This is most likely much more significant than getting the message over. We are meta-imparting - conveying about correspondence!

At the point when we are conversing with an individual, we likewise need to clarify how the substance of our message is to be deciphered. The manner in which we do this says a lot about the relationship we have with this individual, or if nothing else the manner in which we think about this individual. Words can't do this. It is simpler to appear than it is to talk about our feelings. The significance of our words is made through body language.

In the de Sassounian meaning, this langue (in restricted to the parole) is utilized for nonverbal communication. We use it constantly. More often than not we are not by any means mindful of utilizing it. Contacting someone during the discussion implies something totally not the same as not contacting our accomplice in discussion. It is simply unrealistic to convey without utilizing non-verbal language - composed word is the main special case.

Is it true that we are aware?

A large portion of the body language is imparted on an oblivious level. However, it has a broad impact to the nature of our message. From this we can infer that it would be a smart thought to end up aware of our - and what is of much more prominent significance - other's - body language.

We can figure out how to utilize our body language for a reason and to comprehend the body language of others. We additionally must know that body language is deciphered socially - its implications vary in various societies. The understanding relies upon the circumstance, the way of life, the relationship we have with the individual just as the sex of the other. This means not a solitary sign of our body has a similar significance in all pieces of the globe. This is a significant point and ought to be considered. The language of our body is indispensably associated with the communication in language and our total personal conduct standard. With this set up together, different signs can likewise supplement each other to reinforce the importance of what we discuss.

Some social gatherings have built up a particular body

language which is unequivocal in light of the fact that the utilization of words is troublesome in a given circumstance. These are for the most part minority bunches in societies where there is an incredible history of preference of the prevailing society.

Emotions matter

Body language is utilized uniquely to express sentiments. For example, in the event that we are partial to somebody, it is frequently hard to state that straightforwardly to the individual. It is, then again, simpler to make our sentiments obvious (deliberately or inadvertently) through body language. The inverse is additionally valid. We may state that we ARE furious through words, yet our body language might be stating clearly that we are NOT. This can be extremely confounding for the beneficiary of the message. The circumstance is normally portrayed as giving out twofold messages - one message in words and a contrary message in body language. It is additionally hard to lie or conceal our emotions through body language. We may give their actual sentiments away by not monitoring their body language.

Research has indicated that a great many people give more consideration to, and accept all the more promptly, their impression of how an individual demonstrates through body language than what is said through words. As a result, we will put a question mark behind the verbally expressed words if they don't compare with the language of the body.

Consciousness of how we communicate = Vital

Just a little piece of how we go over to someone else is chosen by the words we express (as indicated by research, under 5%). It is of fundamental significance that we know and (to a limited degree) control our body language. The beneficiary of our body language will have an inclination that is regularly hard to portray, to articulate or to demonstrate that something was conveyed. Be that as it may, it was. We have all without a doubt said to ourselves: “I think he/she doesn't care for me” or “I don't generally accept information exchanged.” It is called instinct and body language assumes a major job, as it allows us make signs the other person can interpret at a characteristic level.

We have to become acquainted with our own body

language first. We ought to find out about it with the goal that we can remember it in others just as in ourselves.

➢ Understanding Body Language Concepts

Utilize open body language. This implies you have a self-assured handshake, sit tranquilly, yet radiate vitality, and appear responsible for all signals.

- Your stance ought to be loose, but your back ought to be straight. This shows individuals you are agreeable and sure. Delay when you address attract the audience and show certainty.
- Keep your legs marginally separated so you occupy more room. This likewise shows certainty. Leaning in marginally when an individual is addressing shows enthusiasm (inclining ceaselessly will show a feeling of threatening vibe).
- Don't fold your arms. Rather, let them dangle at your sides or press them together in your lap. This shows you are available to other

individuals.

- Make sure your handshake is firm, but not very squashing. Look at the other individual without flinching, in spite of the fact that you shouldn't gaze excessively. Squint, and turn away in some cases so they don't feel you are attempting to threaten.
- Play with your manner of speaking. The manner of speaking is a way that individuals impart certainty. The way to progress is anticipating certainty.

Recognize passionate body language. You can decide feelings by giving cautious consideration to non-verbal prompts. You ought to likewise take into setting what's happening at the time you detect the enthusiastic signs, however.

- When individuals are furious, their face flushes, they bristle some fur, they grasp their clench hands, and they attack body space, once in a while by inclining forward.

- When individuals are apprehensive or on edge, their face pales, their mouth appears to be dry (so they may lick their lips or drink water), they show shifting discourse tone, and they have strain in their muscles (so they may grasp their arms or hands, and their elbows might be brought into their sides.) Other indications of anxiety incorporate trembling lip, squirming, and wheezing or holding breath.

Abstain from blocking. If you are giving an introduction or discourse, you need to be as open as you can to your crowd. Therefore, you should evacuate physical obstructions that will restrict your capacity to associate.

- Podiums, PCs, seats, and even an envelope are altogether propping that make separation between a speaker and group of spectators, avoiding a feeling of association.

- Crossing your arms or addressing somebody while sitting behind a PC screen are blocking practices.

Spot when somebody is lying. Body language can give away liars. They may have the option to conceal their lies in their words; however, their bodies frequently recount to another story.

- Liars are more averse to keep in touch, and their students may seem choked.
- Turning the body away from you is an indication of lying.
- Complexion changes, for example, redness in the neck or face, and sweat, are generally indications of lying, as are vocal changes.
- Be mindful that a few indications of lying – perspiring, poor or no eye-to-eye connection are additionally signs of anxiety or dread.

Think about spacing. Various societies have various thoughts regarding how much physical space you should give someone else. However, social separation is separated into four classes.

- Intimate separation. Characterized as contacting someone else to 45 centimetres. If you enter an individual's cosy separation, this can be very disrupting for them except if you're invited or you're as of now personal.

- Personal separation. Maintain proxemics to see each other's appearances and signals. 45 centimeters to 1.2 m.
- Social separation. This is the typical separation in circumstances that are generic or business exchanges, characterized as 1.2 m to 3.6 m. Discourse ought to be stronger, and eye-to-eye connection stays significant.
- Public separation. 3.7m to 4.5m. Instances of the individuals who regularly work in open separation are educators or the individuals who converse with individuals in gatherings. Non-verbal correspondence is basic but frequently overstated. Hand signals and head developments can be a higher priority than outward appearances as the last are regularly not seen.

Recognize your body language patterns. Endeavour

to consider what your body is doing in various associations with various individuals. A mirror can be helpful to look at outward appearances and stance, yet primarily you simply need to concentrate on what your body does when you're furious, anxious, or glad.

- Determine whether your body language is in a state of harmony with your message. Your body language is viable in the event that it imparts the message you need it to convey. Does your stance impart certainty, or does it cause you to appear to be uncertain of yourself despite the fact that your words express certainty?

- If your non-verbal sign matches your words, you'll not just convey all the more plainly; you'll likewise be seen as being progressively alluring.

➢ Utilizing Gestures to Communicate

Use hand signals when talking. Specialists accept that individuals who are extraordinary speakers are bound to utilize hand signals during discussions or introductions, and they state hand motions give audience members more noteworthy trust in the speaker.

- More complex motions including two hands over the midsection are related with complex reasoning.
- Politicians like Colin Powell, Barack Obama, Tony Blair, and Bill Clinton are viewed as alluring, powerful speakers, and that is somewhat in light of the fact that they often use hand signals.

Move all through the room. Don't just move your hands. Incredible speakers move around. They point at slides, and they don't stay away from individuals. They are enlivened.

- Your hands being in your pockets when talking or having a discussion will cause you to appear to be unreliable and shut off.
- In contrast, if you remove your hands from your pockets and keep your palms upward, you will show that you are amiable and acceptable.

Spot seals. These are signals that are the counterparts of words. Symbols can be either latent or they can be tolerating. Keep in mind that a few insignias will have various implications to various societies.

- Clenched hands or other pressure in the body can be indications of hostility, as though the individual is set up for a battle. Confronting the other individual, setting things straight and towards them, and sitting close to them can likewise be indications of animosity. Unexpected developments may be made.
- In contrast, tolerating motions are those when the arms are adjusted and palms sideways, as though the individual is presenting a counterfeit embrace. Signals are moderate and delicate. Gesturing when an individual talks shows you concur with them, and causes you to appear to be an incredible audience.

Have great posture. In the event that you go to a prospective employee meeting, and you have an awful stance, you will presumably appear all the more ineffective to the questioner.

- People will connect awful stance with frail certainty or fatigue or absence of commitment. They may even believe you're languid and unmotivated if you don't sit upright.

- To have great stance, your head ought to be up and your back ought to be straight. Lean forward in case you're situated. Plunk down the front of your seat, and lean forward marginally to show you're intrigued and locked in.

Mirror someone else. Mirroring is the point at which one accomplice mirrors the stance of the other accomplice. By replicating the activities of the other individual, you will make them feel associated with you.

- You can mirror an individual's tone, body language or position of the body. You shouldn't do this outrightly or over and over, however, just inconspicuously.

- Mirroring is one of the best approaches to utilize body language to build an affinity with somebody.

Underscore your point with motions. Have more than one motion. This will assist you with communicating better as the need should arise. If you need to ensure you're not misconstrued, rehash the two signals when you talk the thought so anyone might hear.

- If the audience doesn't get on one signal, the individual in question will probably be comfortable with the other. You don't need to utilize a body language signal (or two) for each word; however, it's a smart thought to have a tool kit of motions you can use to fortify significant, yet effectively misjudged ideas.
- Direct the best signals toward the audience. This lets you all the more unmistakably show that you are offering a positive result to the audience. Direct the most negative signals from yourself and the audience. Along these lines, you unmistakably show that you wish that no deterrent disrupts the general flow of your expected message.

Avoid gestures that show anxiety or uncertainty. Keep a check of other body language signals. Watch for meandering eyes, hands picking at your garment, and consistent sneezing.

- Touching one's face signals nervousness. Improve your stance. In case you're continually slouched over or contacting your face, you'll never look sure, congenial or calm. Improving your stance and attempting to wipe out apprehensive tics can be troublesome and will require some serious energy, yet you'll rapidly improve your general non-verbal correspondence.

- These little signals include and are altogether ensured to hose the viability of your message. Try not to stress over if you incidentally play out a couple of these in some random setting.

➢ Interpreting Facial Expressions

Make sense of the "visual strength proportion." When you are conversing with somebody, you should attempt to be the individual who is "outwardly prevailing" to exhibit certainty. This proportion is controlled by making sense of who is taking a gander at the other individual's eyes more, and who is turning away more.

- Your visual strength proportion figures out where you remain on social predominance chain of command contrasted with the other individual in the discussion. Individuals who invest the greater part of the energy turning away have a generally low measure of social strength. Individuals who are less inclined to turn away are most likely the chief.
- People who look down during presentations appear powerless, since they appear as though they are attempting to stay away from analysis or any contention.

Use eye contact to send messages. The windows to the spirit are the eyes, as the banality goes. You can get familiar with a great deal about an individual by focusing on how they utilize their eyes.

- Avoiding eye contact by any means, or looking downward with the eyes a great deal, are the two signs of prevention. Eye-to-eye connection will be increasingly persistent if an individual is attempting to hear you out, as opposed to talk. Turning away from the other individual can likewise be a sign the individual doing the talking isn't prepared to stop and tune in yet.

- Looking at an individual can be a sign of fascination. Individuals who are keen on somebody show healthy eye-to-eye connection and fit forward toward the other individual in the discussion.
- Depending on the unique situation, looking at someone else can be utilized to show regard. For instance, when you're giving an introduction to a room brimming with individuals, partition the room into thirds. Address remarks to the other side, and after that the opposite side, and afterward the centre. Choose an individual in each area to deliver remarks to.

Comprehend influence shows. Give close consideration to outward appearances that pass on feeling, particularly in the event that they struggle with the words an individual is articulating. They can assist you with making sense of an individual's actual feelings.

- Regulators are outward appearances that give criticism during discussions, for example, gesturing the head, and articulations of intrigue or weariness. Controllers enable the other individual to evaluate level of intrigue or understanding. Basically, they give criticism.

- You can show compassion towards someone else by utilizing agreed signals, for example, gesturing your head and grinning. These signals, utilized when someone else is talking, give them encouraging feedback.

- Maintain a strategic distance from prevention. Certain body language motions, including outward appearances, convey prevention, not certainty. Therefore, they cause you to appear to be less in charge.

- Limited outward appearances and little, near the body hand/arm signals indicate protectiveness.

- Turning the body away from the other individual or folding your arms before your body are different signs of protectiveness.

Watch for disengagement. If you are giving an introduction, you need individuals to be locked in. If you are the individual viewing the introduction, you need to appear to be locked in. There are signs you can search for that demonstrate commitment or a deficiency in that department.

- Heads tilted downward and eyes looking somewhere else demonstrate withdrawal.

- Slumping in a seat is an indication of separation. Essentially, fiddling, doodling, or composing are signs that an individual is withdrawn.

CHAPTER FOURTEEN

LIVING WITH A PURPOSE

What is the purpose behind your life? Working, eating and dozing is no life. There must be some great purpose and some respectable aim of your living. If you are living without a purpose, at that point, I am sorry to say, you are carrying on with the life of a creature.

What would you like to accomplish for yourself and for other people? What do you intend to achieve in your life? What might you want to encourage yourself and to others? Rise, look straight in the mirror, open your eyes, and advise yourself the genuine purpose behind your very own life, noisily and plainly.

Try not to carry on with a customary life. Carry on with an overly great life. Carry on with the life of a saint who isn't just being adored by individual people but in addition revered while he is physically no more in this world.

Help yourself by dealing with your body, mind and

soul. Your body needs great sustaining nourishment to stay dynamic, vivacious and savvy. Your spirit needs otherworldly nourishment to stay healthy. Keep your body healthy and cheerful. Invest some peaceful energy in contemplation, supplications and building up an imperceptible contact with your Creator. Upgrade your psychological capacities by perusing some great interesting books, articles and upboosting personal growth material.

Help your family by giving them your own adoration and fondness which they need more than your material help to them. Deal with poor people, old and debilitated people who need some sort of help from you. At the point when somebody is in a difficult situation give them some assistance. This is your ethical commitment. The world can turn into a brilliant place to live if every single person starts caring about other individuals.

The greatest satisfaction of humankind is in sharing and giving. Cheerfully, share your time, cash, nourishment, emotions, considerations and thoughts with your companions, family and associates. Continuously prepare to give whatever you can provide for other people. If you don't have anything else to give, at that point give your grins. Continuously pass on great, empowering and kind comments about others. Now and again, you can change an individual's life for good just by actually promising him.

We would all be able to live with purpose on the grounds that there is such a great amount to live for. There are things we can seek after, find, or achieve that fill our lives with purpose and significance. We can have vision for our dreams, lives, and satisfy our purposes for living. There is continually something for us to do. Seeking after interests, creating abilities, defining objectives, and organizing our time all assist us to develop and give us something to envision. We can make the most of every day and live with purpose.

Our qualities direct our conduct and the manner in which we assess the world. Our qualities figure out what our identity is, the means by which we invest our energy, what's critical to us, our preferences, our mentalities, etc. We settle on choices dependent on our qualities consistently. Once in a while, our qualities strife with one another. For instance, investing energy with our family may struggle with our work routine which requests broad hours. Explaining our qualities encourages us to comprehend which esteems are most essential to us and the needs we provide for them. This will assist us with making choices that are predictable to our qualities and that we are content with.

Survey the rundown of qualities given beneath. Add anything to the rundown that best depicts what is critical to you. You will locate that a few qualities are imperative to you while others are, to some degree, significant or not significant by any stretch of the imagination. Underline the qualities that are fairly significant, and circle the qualities that are imperative to you. Survey the qualities you orbited and note your 3 most significant qualities. Presently ask yourself the accompanying questions:

For what purpose are these qualities imperative to me?

How do my qualities influence the choices I make?

What, assuming any, clashing qualities do I have? How would I manage them?

How do my qualities influence the manner in which I equalize work, rest, and play?

How would I invest my energy every day? Is it predictable with my needs?

Individuals can without much of a stretch defeat their downturn in the event that they get love and supportive comments from others. Thoughtful and kind words are in every case very supportive.

Just those individuals who are living with a purpose for existing are the genuine saints. They are carrying on with a great life past desires for other people. Start carrying on with an important life by living with a purpose. The genuineness of your purpose will lead you to the new statures of acclaim and fortune.

How to Always Live with Purpose

The vast majority of us don't consider the master plan frequently enough. We become involved with all the little minutes and errands and activities of the day, and we centre so hard around them, or they divert us to a great degree, that before the day's over we have a truly narrow-minded perspective on the world and of our lives. How regularly do you keep awake around evening time contemplating your life's purpose, and how frequently would you say you are kept up around evening time considering the little dramatizations of the day? Living with design is an expertise, a propensity it's something that can be developed and created.

Obviously, to live with purpose you should have some thought of what your purpose in life is. I normally prefer to consider this on several levels. To begin with, I consider what the universal usefulness of the majority of this is. I have not concocted an unmistakable answer, yet I find that contemplating this normally and continually assessing how I feel about existence and presence and the world everywhere keeps life in context, and it keeps me preparing to stun the world.

From the greatest of pictures, I begin to consider the purpose behind a person inside the more prominent purpose and significance of the world. As should be obvious, I like to begin general and start working my way down. All things considered, in the event that there's a universal usefulness to the world, at that point the individual is expected to add to this more prominent purpose. If every individual is proposed to add to the more noteworthy purpose, at that point I have to discover a route as a person to satisfy that job.

At exactly that point, I begin to consider what my own purpose in this world is, after I go to a type of terms with a purpose forever and a purpose behind a person inside the world. Presently, my responses to these inquiries continually change in their points of interest; however, as a rule my life's purpose remains the equivalent.

Since I normally have a decent feeling of what my life's purpose is at some random minute because of customary assessment, I'm at that point prepared to live with that purpose. I like to begin the day and help myself to remember why I am here and what I am here to do and what I have to do today to move towards those objectives. I ensure that my day-by-day activities are lined up with my purpose in this world, and I put forth a valiant effort to adjust myself to the world's more noteworthy purpose.

By the day's end, I like to kick back and think about the day. I like to consider what went well, where I lost my direction. I like to consider how to remain deliberately, and I like to consider how I will live nearer to my purpose the following day. Evenings before bed are additionally the occasions when I'm well on the way to begin to assess and reconsider in the way I recently referenced.

Living with purpose all begins with having a purpose. You have to profoundly comprehend and thoroughly study this purpose and everlastingly re-compose it. You have to live in the nearest arrangement you can with this purpose on an everyday level, and pardon yourself when you wreckage up. It is difficult; however it's the best way to live.

CHAPTER FIFTEEN

GOAL SETTING AND PLANNING

Goal and planning are the thing that individuals state they do. However, do they genuinely do it in a way that inspires them to understand their fantasies? In this section, I give you a basic goal and planning approach that works. It will assist you with achieving anything you earnestly need to accomplish in your life.

Not having a goal in life is identical to not realizing where to go when we hit the street. For some it might look courageous. By the by, on a most dire outcome imaginable, we may arrive at a spot where there is no chance to get back and you need to fight what you get for rest of your life. A considerable lot of us would prefer not to arrive at this sort of circumstance in our lives. Lamentably, numerous individuals see no chance to get out of their present not-exactly-attractive lives and proceed to endure for the duration of their lives. But, much to their dismay they can generally leave the hopelessness and lead an existence of wealth and bliss.

Envision that you are planning an excursion to a radiant sea shore; you will begin getting ready everything that makes the outing charming as well as critical. Your whole family or companions who will go with you would be amped up for the while trip and envision the cheerfulness at the sea shore. You may even notice that time passes off quickly, like hours look like minutes and minutes look like seconds.

Interestingly, envision you and your companions leave on an excursion without planning concerning where to go. Like your most noticeably awful bad dream working out, you may end up in no place and you lose your direction and get stuck in a spot where there is no other viable option for you. Your companions start blaming you. You feel defenceless and embarrassed!

Everybody needs planning and should have a complete goal in their lives regarding what they expect to accomplish. Envision where you need to be in a long time from now and start analysing your five-year plan into lumps of one-year transient plans.

Goal Setting and Planning - A Simple

Approach

Personal Vision

This is your vital aspect for making a strong, feasible life plan. Contribute time to consider all that you put stock in and all that you might want your life to be about. Concentrate on what impact you need your life to have on your family, your companions, and everybody you meet.

Note your thoughts in a diary or utilize your PC. Run down anything that has significance to you. Presently work it out or type it in a section or more. Take as much time as is needed and get it perfectly clear.

Your Strengths

Write down the majority of Your Strengths. From that point onward, list any feeble zones.

Presently this is basic - annihilate the rundown of shortcomings and spotlight absolutely on Your Strengths.

After you have Your Personal Vision and Your Strengths obviously characterized it turns out to be anything but difficult to...

Characterize Your Goals and Desired Outcomes

Audit Personal Vision and Your Strengths a couple of times and after that challenge to dream a tad. Concentrate on what you need your life to resemble in the event that you have a boundless stockpile of cash, assets, and time.

Run down anything you might want to have, do, and accomplish. Record the spots you'd like to visit, individuals you might want to meet, things you might want to learn, and encounters you might want to have.

Next, choose one want that you want to achieve rapidly and effectively. Work it out in detail. This will assist you with valuing the intensity of this basic framework.

Your Why

When you recognize what you want to accomplish, characterize Your Why. Consider what it will intend to you when you achieve this unequivocal result. Imagine yourself having finished it. Presently, directly beneath your goal, record whatever achieving this particular goal would intend to you. This is your self-inspirational power for making a move.

Your Massive Plan of Action

Alright, you have what you might want plainly characterized and you know why you want it. Presently ask yourself, "What are the moves that I should make so as to accomplish my result?" Write them out.

Goal setting and planning, encourages you see obviously what you have to do. The way to getting results is making a move. Concentrate on what you have recorded and pick what you can do right away. Making predictable move is the key fixing that gets results. At the point when you get moving energy becomes an integral factor. You will achieve your particular result and make the most of Your Why.

Put this uncomplicated goal setting and planning framework vigorously for each result you have recorded. Put aside a period consistently to utilize this procedure and make a move each day.

Over the long haul, you will be astounded at how a lot of your life is winding up better.

The Importance of Goal and planning

In the event that you need to arrive at any degree of accomplishment in your life, it is important that you define goals and make arrangements. At the point when you set the goal and make the arrangement to accomplish a specific thing, that gives you a reasonable vision. A reasonable vision implies you know precisely what it is you need to achieve.

Mentors don't simply send their players out on the play field without first setting up an arrangement. So, can any anyone explain why we experience life now and then and not have an unmistakable vision with respect to what we ask for from it?

Defining the goal and making the arrangement plants a dream in your psyche and furthermore your subliminal personality. During this procedure, the subliminal personality is given a lot of guidelines to pursue and complete. It's normal if your arrangement changes every now and then inasmuch as you keep your mind concentrated on the goal. By doing so the arrangement will at last succeed.

To prevail in life, you should set your goals, get an

arrangement, tail it and remain centred. It is critical to stay centred or you'll lose locate. When you dismiss the goal, you will disregard the arrangement and in a little while everything will self-destruct. Why would that be? Since when you quit concentrating on the goal, you are telling your inner mind that the goal is never again significant. Thus, the subliminal personality quits chipping away at making your specific goal a reality.

Staying centre isn't a simple undertaking. Your psyche resembles its very own individual, as though it is totally isolated from you. Despite the fact that you might need to do, be and accomplish a specific thing, your mind will need to keep accomplishing things the manner in which it is used to. It will be obstinate and set up an extraordinary battle. Your mind will give all of you sorts of opposition, even guide you to abandon your fantasies.

So how would you get your brain to tune in and consent to changes? By being constant and remaining submitted by continually thinking about your goals. Search for chances to grasp and invite change. Ensure that you set practical goals. Start little and recognize and commend your little triumphs continually.

At last, your mind will start to comprehend and acknowledge the progressions, and before you know it, your psyche is working with the procedure and the cycle of your goals turning into a reality has begun. Defining goals, getting an arrangement and remaining centred rises to progress.

When last did you consider setting a goal?

What life-changing goal can you set and plan to motivate yourself?

Commit yourself right now!

What?	
By when ?	

What?	
By when?	
What?	
By when?	

CHAPTER SIXTEEN
ESSENTIAL FACTORS FOR MAINTAINING HEALTHY SELF-ESTEEM

High/Healthy self-esteem is fundamentally feeling positive about yourself and esteeming yourself accurately. This can be kept up by outside components, for example, guardians, educators, and mentors among others. These are individuals who give a positive input even in difficult circumstances which could have been considered as a disappointment.

Mainstays of keeping up healthy self-esteem.

Self-esteem can be expanded and kept up through energy. Coming up next are simply the principle mainstays of liking yourself.

1. Individual uprightness - Without the act of individual trustworthiness, you might be sure but not have the feeling of what your thoughts, convictions, and guidelines are to use as a reason for estimating how you

are performing. Respectability comes when individuals' practices coordinate their favoured qualities or when practices and goals coordinate. Trustworthiness assists individuals with assessing themselves.

2. Self-control. According to Lao-tzu, "Individuals who order others are ground-breaking, yet the individuals who have aced themselves are all the more dominant. Individuals can't achieve absolute mindfulness and illuminate without appropriate order and practice." Self-discipline empowers individuals to adapt to difficulties of life. With self-restraint, one can extend outcomes into the future by intuition and arranging.

3. Living purposefully. This is a situation whereby one uses their forces to accomplish objectives. Objectives could be distinctive, for example, examining, building a family, supporting a relationship or in any event, tackling an issue. Through objectives, self-esteem can be raised since it's our objectives that lead us forward and stimulate our reality.

4. Self-assertiveness. Assertiveness is fundamentally acting and doing everything from your deepest feelings and emotions. The significance of this column is for one

to be genuine. Acting from themselves and not duplicating other. Doing what they feel is correct yet not what others think.

5. Self-responsibility. Responsibility is having the option to hold on what you are certain about. Not fleeing due to dread of conviction but representing reality and accepting it. At the point when you react to life challenges, you are dependable.

6. Self-acceptance. This is getting oneself and connecting with issues to discover arrangements in a positive manner. When you acknowledge yourself, you will stay by your life standards of taking the positives and leaving the negatives. In this way, self-acknowledgment is a decent method to help self-esteem.

Do This!

- Stop your internal analysis - This is simply the best point to begin building your fearlessness once more. Quit scrutinizing yourself in everything that you do. Self-analysis leads individuals to simply accomplishing things that please others with the end goal for them to feel acknowledged as opposed to making the right decision. This leads those to begin feeling horrendous about themselves, hence the internal detest start. Evade the inward analysis by reprimanding it. Do what you feel better and see the inspiration as opposed to the cynicism.

- Use healthy inspiration habits - Make the internal voice frail by engaging in activities that raise your regard. This should be possible by concentrating on doing what you truly prefer to do, helping yourself to remember the significance and advantages of accomplishing explicit objectives and guaranteeing self-consolation by accepting negatives as an improvement point.
- Write three things you acknowledge about yourself - Observing in any event three things you love about yourself consistently improves your self-esteem.

CONCLUSION

Keep in mind, self-esteem is identified with the manner in which we think about ourselves, and our existence. By having an increasingly inspirational standpoint and point of view on life, self-esteem can develop, and we can likewise turn out to be physically more advantageous. We can build self-esteem through exercise, reading motivational books like this, defining goals and, above all, by positive self-talk. Two basic components to building your self-esteem are to define goals and make another propensity for speculation decidedly. By deducing distinctly and defining goals, we will be more joyful with our lives and our self-esteem will develop.

A fruitful procedure to develop self-esteem is to compose goals on paper and begin to compose a diary. By burrowing down profoundly to interface with your internal identity, your self-esteem can improve. Journaling is an astounding method to interface with your internal identity.

At the point when you write in your diary, compose

your objectives and be determined to accomplish them. Thinking of them will bring them alive so you can continue rehashing your objectives over and over. The way toward rehashing your objectives routinely empowers your psyche and cerebrum to relearn past negative idea examples substituting them with positive contemplations.

As you begin to encounter achievement in your objectives, definitely, you will rest easy thinking about yourself. This procedure can likewise ease pressure and help forestall coronary illness.

Replacing your negative self-converse with positive self-converse can set you on the correct way to accomplishment in the area of your life you need to see changes.

Printed in Great Britain
by Amazon